A

TEACHER'S
TALE

175 YEARS OF SCOTCH WHISKY
THROUGH THE EYES OF WM TEACHER & SONS

HELEN ARTHUR

First published in Great Britain in 2005 by Allied Domecq Spirits and Wine (UK) Limited.

Copyright © 2005 Allied Domecq Spirits and Wine (UK) Limited.

The right of Helen Arthur to be identified as the author of this work has been asserted in accordance with the Copyright, Designs and Patents Act of 1988.

Designer: Craig Stevens, Butler and Tanner
Printed in the UK by Butler and Tanner, Caxton Road, Frome, Somerset, BA11 1NF

ISBN-10: 0-9551527-0-4
ISBN-13: 978-0-9551527-0-2

Price £25

ACKNOWLEDGEMENTS

The idea for producing this Teacher's 175th Anniversary book was conceived following research and cataloguing of the company archives. These are currently at Glasgow University Archives, at Kilmalid, Ardmore and Glendronach Distilleries. I discovered that the company has one of the most complete histories of a brand in the industry. It also has a unique record of advertising material covering most of the Teacher brand's history and believed it would make a fitting tribute to 'Old Thorough' – William Teacher.

I would personally like to thank Bill Bergius, the present member of the Teacher dynasty working for the company, for his friendship and support, without which this book could not have been written.

Thanks also to Rachel Hosker and the rest of the team at Glasgow University Archives for their assistance, Lorna Sherriff at Glendronach Distillery, Christopher Lumgair, Archivist at the London Sketch Club and other members of the Teacher/Bergius dynasty including Ronnie Anderson for his assistance with the Family Tree.

A Dictionary of Methodism in Britain & Ireland edited by John A Vickers
A Family of Spirit by Geoffrey E Cousins
Cecil Aldin, The Story of a Sporting Artist by Roy Heron
Chambers Poetical Works of Robert Burns edited by William Wallace
Chartist Movement in Britain, 1838-1850 edited by George Claeys, Pickering & Chatto
Great British Wrecks Volume Two by Kendall McDonald
Highland Clearances Memorial Fund
Make your Own Scotch Whisky by Adam Bergius
Reminiscences 1893-1938 by Walter Manera Bergius
Scotch Whisky A Liquid History by Charles Maclean
Scotch Whisky An Illustrated Guide by J Marshall Robb BSc
The History of the Incorporation of Maltmen in Glasgow by Craig Mair BA DSA Scot
The Ingenious Mr Bell 1767-1830 Pioneer of Steam Navigation by Brian D Osborne
The Spirit of Glasgow, The Story of Teacher's Whisky by Edward Chisnall
The Scotch Whisky Industry Record by H Charles Craig
The Triumph of Reform Halevy's History of the English People 1830-1841 by Elie Halevy
The Whisky Distilleries of the United Kingdom by Alfred Barnard
Wallace Milroy's Malt Whisky Almanac

Helen Arthur

CONTENTS

"I wonder why he always brings his own?"

Every time we invite him round he turns up with a bottle of Teacher's and starts running down my budget Scotch.

Every time he comes he goes on and on about how Teacher's is a family blend, still produced by the same family in the traditional way. And how all that makes Teacher's such a smooth mellow Scotch, unlike my budget brand.

Then he keeps on insisting I try it. And then when, for the sake of peace and quiet, I do, he has the cheek to complain I've drunk the lot.

Surely he doesn't expect me to get my Teacher's out?

He'll never learn.

Teacher's. The cream of Highland whiskies.

FOREWORD

In the Teacher family, life and energy are in the blood as surely as there is strength and spirit in a glass of the same name.

This is the story of a family and whisky, put in the context of its 175 years. The river flows, but the stones remain. Generations of the Teacher family pass, but the character and the spirit stay true to this day.

It is about an energetic family who distilled wood, coal and barley, built cars, engines and ships, and fabricated other engineering projects. The story touches on the success of private enterprise in the face of larger capital resources of an international scale.

My father, Walter Bergius, was Managing Director of Teacher's for a generation. He was profoundly deaf, but this disability never deterred him in business, family or sporting life. Its effect was to concentrate his sense of good order and perfection. As I read again about William Teacher and the family, I recognise inherited characteristics.

Finally to Helen Arthur who has generously advised me at Teacher's over the past 17 years. As painter, writer and historian, she embraces the spirit of William Teacher.

Bill Bergius
Great great grandson of William Teacher, Founder of Teacher's whisky

FAMILY TREE

WILLIAM TEACHER (OLD THOROUGH)
BORN 5/6/1811
DIED 27/12/1876
M. AGNES McDONALD 1834

WILLIAM TEACHER JNR
BORN 28/11/1836
DIED 12/04/1880
M. ELIZABETH ANNE CURTIS
BORN 5/6/1861

JOHN

ADAM
BORN 10/2/1839
DIED 31/12/1898

CATHERINE

DONALD
BORN 9/8/1849
DIED DEC 1883
M. CELIA NORTON LAW

CHRISTINA

ELLEN McDONALD
BORN 12/3/1862
M. JOHN STEVENSON

JOHN HAMMOND
BORN 25/10/1869
DIED 21/11/1919

MABEL LIZZIE
BORN 7/12/1871
DIED 11/5/1947
M. JOHN HUTCHESON

AGNES McDONALD
BORN 11/11/1874
DIED 16/7/1954

WILLIAM CURTIS TEACHER
BORN 6/8/1863
DIED 20/1/1929
M. ELIZABETH ROWENA McNAIRN 1889

WILLIAM GEORGE TEACHER
BORN 17/12/1893
KILLED IN ACTION
14/5/1916

MAUDE ROWENA
BORN 6/8/1895
M. ROBERT JACK DUNLOP

NORA HELEN CURTIS
BORN 22/1/1899
M. ALASTAIR (ALFIE) C J M ANDERSON

RONALD McNAIRN TEACHER
BORN 7/12/1900
DIED 17/9/1975

GEORGE TEACHER DUNLOP
BORN 27/5/1923
DIED 24/1/1992
M. JANE SCHOELLES

ROBERT J DUNLOP
BORN 2/7/1927
M. SHIRLEY DIXON

RONALD GRAHAM GRAY ANDERSON
BORN 3/6/1933
M. EVELYNE SOCQUET-CLERC

Key members are highlighted in orange for W^M Teacher & Sons history.

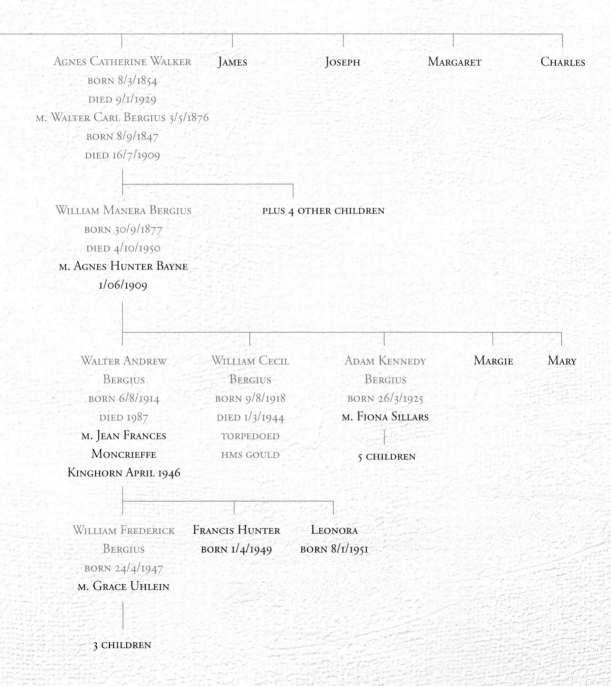

AGNES CATHERINE WALKER   JAMES   JOSEPH   MARGARET   CHARLES

BORN 8/3/1854

DIED 9/1/1929

M. WALTER CARL BERGIUS 3/5/1876

BORN 8/9/1847

DIED 16/7/1909

WILLIAM MANERA BERGIUS   PLUS 4 OTHER CHILDREN

BORN 30/9/1877

DIED 4/10/1950

M. AGNES HUNTER BAYNE

1/06/1909

WALTER ANDREW   WILLIAM CECIL   ADAM KENNEDY   MARGIE   MARY

BERGIUS   BERGIUS   BERGIUS

BORN 6/8/1914   BORN 9/8/1918   BORN 26/3/1925

DIED 1987   DIED 1/3/1944   M. FIONA SILLARS

M. JEAN FRANCES   TORPEDOED

MONCRIEFFE   HMS GOULD   5 CHILDREN

KINGHORN APRIL 1946

WILLIAM FREDERICK   FRANCIS HUNTER   LEONORA

BERGIUS   BORN 1/4/1949   BORN 8/1/1951

BORN 24/4/1947

M. GRACE UHLEIN

3 CHILDREN

ESTD
WM TEACHER & SONS
GLASGOW
1830

CHAPTER ONE

TEACHER'S HIGHLAND CREAM

The proverbial message in a bottle starts with the discovery of the bottle.

There's a robustness and maturity about a bottle of Teacher's Highland Cream Scotch Whisky. William Teacher, the founder, was said to be a robust, uncompromising man seeking ultimate perfection. Yet, this is still only half the story, for the bottle also reflects the fact that William was straightforward, believed implicitly in what he did, wasn't afraid to stick his neck out when he thought it necessary and looked for new opportunities whenever he could. All the while William ensured that the brand that bore his name was of the highest quality and remained entirely unaltered.

The Teacher's Highland Cream bottle has changed very little over the past 92 years (see pictures below). The shape is roughly the same, sometimes a little sleeker, but still quite heavy in appearance. The cap, too, has changed over time from the cork in 1913 to a jigger (or measure cap) in 1967 and the pilfer-proof closure in 1987. This bottle tells you that there is nothing gimmicky about Teacher's Highland Cream or Wm Teacher & Sons Ltd. No compromises – there never have been, there never will be.

The labels show a simple branding statement without any pictures. What you see is what you get. And what you still get is one of the highest malt-content, premium-blended Scotch whiskies on the market today. And that is exactly what you would have received when William Teacher first put his own blended whisky in a bottle in the 1850s.

BUY ONE DON'T GET ONE FREE!

What do you think we are, a charity? It's not that we're mean spirited. Indeed, it's the generously high malt content of our blend that gives our whisky its distinctive taste. The same way it's always been, since 1862. But then to suggest that we just start giving it away willy-nilly, well, that's simply ridiculous.

SCOTCH. THE WAY WE LIKE IT.

DRINKAWARE.CO.UK ENJOY RESPONSIBLY

To celebrate the company's 175th anniversary the bottle has been redesigned, but the strength of character and styling remains (see pictures above). The key changes are the black cap and the lower part of the front label, which is gold reversed out of black. This design echoes some of the Teacher's advertising in the 1930s (see picture opposite). There have been changes, but the integrity of the pack is one that William Teacher would immediately recognise as his own.

To understand the man who created Teacher's Highland Cream it is necessary to go back to the very beginning; to learn more about the world in which he was born and grew up in, and in which he and his family were to shape their own special way.

Behind every great idea, whether it's in the world of industry or business or the arts, there's a great individual. In the case of Wm Teacher & Sons there was the leader, "Old Thorough" (1811-1876), who left his mark and was followed by sons, a son-in-law, grandchildren and great-grandchildren and a great-great-grandchild, all of whom made their own significant contributions.

WILLIAM TEACHER: BIRTH, APPRENTICESHIP, SOCIAL REFORM AND MARRIAGE

Let's return to the year 1811 in the town of Bridge of Weir, west of Paisley, Scotland, on a June morning. It is summer so the day dawns very early. Yet even now the textile factories are working and the sound of boiling vats, flying shuttles and the clacking of looms can be heard all over the town. People have left their homes before first light and have stumbled through the dirty cobble-stoned streets to work. For this is 1811 when conditions were rough and life was hard: domestic coal fires and industrial smoke fouled the air; the first gas lights were only installed a decade later, in 1823; and it was before the first Factory Acts had created a safer environment for workers.

But at one house on this particular morning of 5 June, the residents are probably only aware of one small cry, announcing the birth of a new baby, to be christened William.

William Teacher's parents weren't rich – his father was a sailor and his mother Margaret worked in the local mill as a pieceworker – and the world couldn't have looked particularly bright for this small baby. But there were things going on in the outside world, which were to shape William's future, and that of the country into which he had been born.

(Seven years earlier in 1804, in Berlin, Germany, young Karl Julius Bergius was born; he was to become an engineer. His son Walter was to forge a very special link with William Teacher by marrying his youngest daughter.)

Separating fact from fiction isn't always easy. With William Teacher, however, there is quite a lot of written material. The first source is a detailed Bergius Family Tree, which was revised and extended by William Manera Bergius in Glasgow, in May 1905, and further added to by Walter Andrew Bergius, again in Glasgow, in October 1955. This confirms William's birth as,

> *"5 June 1811 at Bridge of Weir. His father was drowned at sea, before he was a year old. His mother worked in the spinning mills, and in his seventh year he worked with her as piecer. At 11 he became apprentice tailor with Robert Barr."*

In addition to *The Bergius Family Tree* there is an account by Agnes McDonald Teacher, who was William Teacher's granddaughter.

> *"To return to William Teacher, Senior – as a small boy he lived with his mother (nee Margaret Fram or Frame) at Duntocher and to earn a little, I suppose, he used to go out with tailor Robert Barr to farms, helping with the sewing and suchlike, and as they walked Barr taught the intelligent boy and so laid the foundation of his love of books and learning generally which cause him later to give his family the best*

education he could find. Eventually he gave tailor Barr, who went to America, a pension. Rather amusingly, it was found that tailor Barr was still drawing his pension when he would have been over 100."

After some research the archives do not support this final statement, but it does make a good story.

This meant that after the death of her husband, Margaret Teacher had left Bridge of Weir and travelled across the Clyde to Duntocher to live and work. The yearly average wages for skilled labour such as a coalminer, factory worker or school-teacher was around £20, but mill pieceworkers, such as Margaret, would have earned much less.

The early 19th century was a tough time for the people of Scotland. The Napoleonic Wars (1803-1815) and the French grain blockade meant that many went hungry. The demand for food placed increasing stress on the land and landowners found a devastating way of achieving higher production. In particular, the prices of lamb and wool rose dramatically and to increase flocks landowners started clearing as many tenant farmers as they could from their land. This replacement of people with sheep was seen by the landowners as "Improvements", but not surprisingly by the tenant farmers as "Clearances". The history of these "Improvements" goes way back to the middle of the 18th century. For years, absentee landowners had no regard for the people who worked their land; they simply wanted to make as much money as they could from their estates.

One example is Elizabeth Gordon, Countess of Sutherland, who started clearing people from her estates in 1810. She usually lived in London with her husband and rarely visited Sutherland. They employed a lawyer, Patrick Sellar, and a factor called James Lock to remove the farmers. This they did brutally, without any concern for the welfare of the farmers and their families – injuries often resulted in death or maiming. Over 2,000 homes a day were burned during

Teacher's logo early 1900s printing block.

Bury the Corkscrew
campaign 1913
printing block.

the Clearances. Many of these crofts had been occupied by the same family for as long as 500 years. Left with no shelter, people literally starved and froze to death. Some of those who were able to escape the tyranny of the landlords left Scotland to work overseas.

Others were forcibly evicted and sent to the Colonies against their will. In 1826 MacLean of Coll, who owned the Isle of Rhum, paid £5 14s. for each adult on his land to emigrate to Canada. As many as 300 people were evicted from his estate in this way. As Chieftain of the Clan he had ceased to be the father figure, the provider and someone to respect, and had instead become the oppressor. The old Clan values had been changed forever.

Unlike the huge bustling city of today, Glasgow was then a small traditional burgh where everyone knew everyone else and their business and the craftsmen and merchants dominated the social scene. But this was changing and the population had almost doubled from 66,000 in 1791 to 116,000 in 1811. Industry was creating new opportunities and the city needed to improve its communications with the outside world. During the 1770s work started on increasing the depth of the River Clyde, which until then had not been able to accept large ships. In 1806 Thomas Telford's plan to open up the river by canalising it and building a retaining wall was nearly complete.

The start of a new age began in 1811. Trials for Henry Bell's first steamship, the *Comet*, were under way. This paddle-steamer made its maiden voyage in August 1812. On Monday 10 August the *Glasgow Herald* reported as follows:

> *"We understand that a beautiful and commodious boat has just been finished, constructed to go by wind-power and steam, and for carrying passengers on the Clyde between Glasgow, Port Glasgow, Greenock and Garrock. On Thursday it arrived at the Broomielaw in three hours and a half from Port Glasgow."*

Bell was landlord of the Baths Inn in Helensburgh 35km (22 miles) downriver from Glasgow, which he had set up so that the wealthy people of Glasgow could visit for salt-water baths. The trip to his hotel took some six hours over rough terrain, so providing a shorter, more comfortable journey by river was certainly in his own interests. In 1818 the *Comet* started a regular service between Glasgow and Fort William via the Crinan Canal. This only lasted two years as the boat was wrecked off Craignish Point on 15 December 1820.

With the introduction of steam-powered vessels, journey times were greatly reduced and overseas markets were to become a real possibility for the new industries in Glasgow and the surrounding towns. Not only was steam to replace sail, but steel was replacing wood and new engineering miracles were being achieved daily. Down south King George III was on the throne and, across the Channel in 1812, Napoleon was struggling towards Moscow.

When William started working at the mill in 1818 young children were forced to work extremely long hours. At the beginning of the 19th century members of the Evangelicals, who were strongly represented throughout the middle classes, started pressing for reform. The first Act, which was drafted principally by the Evangelicals and attempted to control the apprenticeship of pauper children to mill owners, was passed in 1802. This had relatively little effect as no inspection mechanism was incorporated.

Finding out more about Robert Barr, the tailor, has so far proved impossible. The name Barr was an important one in the area and a large linen-weaving concern in Paisley also went under the name of Robert Barr. The National Archive Collection has records covering the history of this linen mill until 1806. It could be that the company ceased trading in 1806 for there was a shift at this time from Scotland down to Lancashire where new cotton mills, in particular, were opening up every day. Was William's Robert Barr a relation of this mill owner? We will probably never know the answer.

By 1821, when William was 10, the population of Glasgow had increased to 142,000 and was growing. It was no longer the large friendly burgh of the late 1770s and the emphasis had changed so that large businesses and industries were in control.

After five years working for Robert Barr, William went back to the mills and worked as a cotton spinner. From the age of 16 William appears to have been a bit of a rebel and he joined the Chartist Movement. In 1827 the Chartist Movement was starting to influence the political scene and was determined by reform to improve the economic and social conditions of the industrial working classes. William grew up during the key years of the Movement and this was to have a lasting impression on him.

The Bergius Family Tree continues:

> *"At sixteen he started cotton spinning, at the same time joining the ranks of the Chartists. During the riots it was he who hoisted the Reform flag on the roof of the mill at Duntocher, and he only escaped a sentence of penal servitude, the fate of the six ringleaders, because of his youth."*

There is clearly some discrepancy here, for at 16 William would have been considered a man and would probably not have escaped a sentence of some kind. It is far more likely that the mill owner or somebody else intervened on his behalf. But the reason above is far more romantic!

Agnes McDonald Teacher, William's granddaughter, described him as "the tall 6ft red-haired callant", and perhaps his fiery temperament could be put down to this! Most photographs of William Teacher show him in his old age with a grim expression, a huge beard and wearing a greatcoat. However, the photograph of him as a young man (opposite) shows him to be good looking with a fine face – it is difficult to confirm or deny whether the hair is red or not; perhaps auburn would be a better description.

Throughout 1830 and 1831 protests for better living and working conditions were made in both the agricultural and burgeoning manufacturing sectors. This unrest led to a Factories Inquiry Commission and reform was spurred on by the activities of reactionaries such as Harriet Martineau, Henry Brougham and Robert Owen. William took a great interest in improving working and living conditions and it is evident that in later life he took his beliefs into the workplace for he was seen as a fair and responsible employer. The Martineaus and others fighting for reform were to become personal friends.

Finally, in 1834, the Reform Act was passed. This legislated that children under 13 years of age should work no more than eight hours a day and children under 18 no more than ten hours a day. In addition, children whose working week was restricted to 48 hours had to attend school every day for two hours. Whilst well intentioned this final piece of legislation was seriously flawed. Children's incomes were reduced, as no state funding supported their education and manufacturers took the cost of schooling out of their wages. Trade unions started to spring up and Robert Owen founded the Grand National Trades Union, which petitioned for an eight-hour day for everyone, a totally unsuccessful objective.

The next key date in William's life is 1832 when he married Agnes McDonald. Agnes McDonald Teacher takes over the story here:

> *"How … Agnes McDonald met her future husband was, as follows, told to me by my mother and so authentic. William Teacher at that time was in the linen (or cotton)*

business. One evening a friend took him to the house of some friends of his. They much enjoyed the company of the lively Mrs McDonald (nee Nancy Stewart) and her three daughters. As they came away, William said, 'I know who I am going to marry.' 'Indeed you're not', exclaimed the other, 'I am going to marry her', and then was greatly relieved to hear it was 'the wee dark one' that Willie had fallen in love with. At that time Agnes was engaged to a comfortably off widower, largely to please her parents, but the tall 6ft red-haired callant won the day."

A GROWING FAMILY, WHISKY SHOPS AND WALTER BERGIUS

There now seem to be two stories of the events of the next few years. The first is of a reasonably long courtship and that William started working for Agnes' mother, Mrs McDonald, in her grocer's shop and through his efforts they had diversified into wines and spirits by 1830. Agnes McDonald Teacher (William's granddaughter) relates that Agnes McDonald's father, *"had something to do with weights and measures and was known for his integrity. He did not believe in 'followers' and was usually off to bed before visitors arrived."*

Agnes McDonald Teacher's story continues:

"A number of years later, to help with the growing family, Agnes started a grocer's shop which was very successful as she was capable, 'natty' or 'dainty' in her ways. The cotton spinning having largely left Glasgow for Lancashire her husband, after a time, gave up his business and joined her – and so was started the first place of business – William Teacher & Sons."

The Bergius Family Tree indicates, too, that Agnes McDonald was a woman of enterprise and reports:

"He [William] wished to emigrate to America, and in order to make money quickly his wife started a grocer's shop, which was so successful that he soon gave up cotton spinning and joined in it, adding wines and spirits. But the money saved for emigration was given to start a Reform newspaper for the amelioration of the condition of the working classes and to pay for the defence of the Chartist leaders."

This could imply that William Teacher didn't start in the grocer's shop until after his marriage to Agnes in 1832, but company records show that they were dealing in whisky before then. This must have been a really exciting time for William and his young wife embarking on a career selling whisky. This was a relatively new industry and he was certainly a pioneer.

The first Teacher shop opened in Piccadilly Street, Anderston. By 1836, the Glasgow Post Office Directories show, "1836–37: William Teacher, Spirit Dealer, 50 Cheapside Street". Cheapside Street is also in Anderston and this could well be William's second shop.

Now we have William ensconced in his grocer's shop it is time to look at the world of whisky, which was to shape his future. The first Glasgow-based whisky distillery was opened in 1784 by Baillie William Menzies in Kirk Street, Gorbals, and by 1825 there were at least nine more in the City.

By the time William started trading in whisky in the early 1830s there were at least 64 Scottish, 21 Irish and two English whisky distilleries operating. (These figures have been established by going through *The Scotch Whisky Industry Record* by H. Charles Craig (1994) and Alfred Barnards's book *The Whisky Distilleries of the United Kingdom* (1887) They list distilleries, which were either properly registered at the time or which survived after the passing of the 1823 Excise Act.) There would have been many more distilleries operating illegally throughout Scotland. Some of them – such as Ardbeg, Glendronach, Laphroaig, Balblair, Glenburgie, Glencadam, Milton Duff and Pulteney – are working today and have belonged, or still do belong, to Allied Domecq.

The Glendronach Distillery nestling in the countryside near Huntly was purchased by Teacher's in 1960.

In the early 19th century Highland distillers depended on malted barley for their make, whilst other cereals were used by the larger Lowland distillers. There was plenty of whisky to choose from. With the introduction of the 1823 Excise Act, good-quality whisky was more freely available and supply was not dependent on smuggling activities. This Act meant that distillers could produce whisky to their own recipes and of a far better quality.

Ardbeg: one of the whiskies available to William Senior when he started in business in 1830.

There was no longer the need to build stills, which could be dismantled easily and hidden from the Exciseman. William showed considerable enterprise by seizing the opportunity to create a new business offering carefully chosen whiskies from the now legal distilleries.

(The 1823 Excise Act was to change the way distilleries worked and pave the way for today's whisky industry. License fees remained at £10, duty was cut to 2s5d a gallon of spirits produced, with a rebate for distillers using the more expensive malted barley.)

William also started his own business when Scotland seemed to have been rediscovered by writers and poets. The exciseman turned poet, Robbie Burns (1759–96), had started the trend and his poems are now inextricably linked to whisky and all things Scottish:

> *"Let other poets raise a fracas*
> *'Bout vines, an' wines, an' drucken Bacchus*
> *An' crabbet names an' stories wrack us,*
> *An' grate our lug*
> *I sing the juice Scotch bere can mak us,*
> *In glass or jug.*
>
> *O thou, my muse! Guid auld Scotch drink!*
> *Whether thro' wimplin worms thou jink,*
> *Or, richly brown, realm owre the brink,*
> *In glorious faem,*

Inspire me, till I lisp an' wink,
To sing thy name!

Let husky wheat the haughs adorn,
An' aits set up their awnie horn,
An' pease and beans, at e'en or morn,
Perfume the plain:
Leeze me on thee, John Barleycorn,
Thou king o'grain!"

Scotch Drink

(John Barleycorn is a reference to the grain barley, which is used to make whisky.)

In another poem, Burns describes the making of whisky including cutting of the barley, laying the grains out on the malting floor, drying and grinding the malted barley:

"Then let us toast John Barleycorn,
Each man a glass in hand:
And may his great posterity
Ne'er fail in old Scotland!"

John Barleycorn – A Ballad

In the "Tale of Tam O'Shanter", (a further reference to this poem appears later in this book) Robert Burns writes about,

"Inspiring bold John Barleycorn!
What dangers thou canst make us scorn!
Wi' tippenny we fear nae evil;
Wi' usquabae we'll face the devil!"

(Tippenny is a reference to a weak beer, which was sold at 2d. a Scots pint. Usquabae is Gaelic for the water of life, or Whisky.)

Sir Walter Scott (1771–1832) with the Waverley Novels, among other books, continued to popularise the beauty of the Scottish highlands, glens, valleys, lochs and castles. Also, down south in England, another writer Charles Dickens (1812–70) was starting to publish his novels. These, written in an amusing and incisive style, dealt with topics of social injustice, poverty and crime. As Dickens' books such as *Great Expectations*, *David Copperfield* and *The Old Curiosity Shop* were widely published, many initially in instalments, it is not implausible to speculate that William would have read them and empathised with their aims.

Advertisement for USA market circa 1976.

William Senior and Agnes had a total of 11 children. The eldest, John, was born on 17 March 1835 but sadly died of scarlet fever whilst on holiday at Helensburgh in 1851. The second, William Junior, born on 28 November 1836, was to become a partner in Wm Teacher & Sons, together with his younger brother Adam, who was born on 10 February 1839.

The first daughter, Catherine, was born in 1841, followed by two brothers, James in 1843, and Joseph in 1845. Margaret followed next in 1847, then Donald in 1849, who later worked in the firm of Wylie, Gordon and Teacher in London. Christina was born in 1850, then Charles Clarke in 1852 and finally, on 8 March 1854, Agnes Catherine Walker.

Agnes McDonald Teacher relates that as part of her grandfather's wishes his children were given the best possible education, "His four daughters were at boarding school in Germany and two at Brussels at Madame Vents". This explains why two daughters married foreigners. Catherine married Gustave Peltzer of Rheydt in 1862 and Christina married Paul Schott, also of Rheydt, in 1870. It was not only the girls who received a good education, for Charles was to become a physician in Edinburgh.

William Teacher's early learning at the side of Robert Barr was to kindle a thirst for knowledge. As *The Bergius Family Tree* relates:

> *"This was the foundation of William Teacher's life-long love of literature and accurate knowledge. At 54 he started learning French and, at 60, German. He was a member of the Unitarian Church, then more than unpopular, and was for many years treasurer and trustee. He interested himself in every movement for toleration and freedom. At his simple and hospitable house in Holland Place, Glasgow, he entertained many men and women of note in the more advanced religious and scientific world, among whom were Harriet and James Martineau, the Faucets, Charpentier, Mazzini and Emerson."*

Karl Julius Bergius, Walter Carl's father, was a Doctor of Philosophy in Berlin. He specialised in law and finance and became Councillor for the German Government in Breslau in 1839. He argued for the reform of the Prussian Constitution and corresponded with some of the leading thinkers and reformers at that time. This created a link with the American Hugh McCulloch and Harriet and James Martineau. It is therefore not surprising that when Walter Carl came to Scotland he should look up William Teacher. This led to romance and Walter married William's youngest daughter Agnes Catherine Walker Teacher in 1876.

Walter Carl Bergius left Germany at the age of 19 to escape the oppression of the new German Empire. Here *The Bergius Family Tree* takes over:

> *"He left Zwinger College with an 'excellent' leaving certificate and served his apprenticeship in a Rostock shipyard, after which, to quality for managership, he made several voyages as a carpenter in the Rostock barque Mathilde, and later on as*

engineer in the Hamburg-America liner Westphalia. In fulfilment of his obligation of military service he joined the Shipyard Division of Kiel. It turned out, however, that the workshops were as yet unfinished; hence his duties in the navy being nominal, he joined the university course of higher mathematics and was employed as one of the unpaid assistants of Kiel Observatory. His connection with this famous establishment led him at a later period to take up astronomy as a pursuit. He delivered a course of astronomical lectures at the Edinburgh Athenaeum and a more extended one at the Andersonian College (West of Scotland Technical College), Glasgow; and acted as first President of the West of Scotland Branch of the British Astronomical Association.

"His connection with Glasgow dates back to 1866, when he was assistant draughtsman to James Howden and afterwards to Randolph Elder & Co. His linguistic qualifications lifted him out of subordinate service in the drawing office, and he was employed in contracting for Marko Negoro's sugar mill at Sourabaya, and as surveyor in the building of the Sirius and Canopus on Bremen account.

"He married Agnes Catherine Walker at Glasgow 3rd May 1876.

"Between 1869 and 1905 Walter Carl B. and W. C. Bergius & Co contracted for the La Flandre for Antwerp, the Rapido and the Humayta for Brazil, the Kobe for Japan and the Bonnie Doon for Stettin owners. They were associated with T. Ciervo in the construction of the Barcelona gasworks and with the Naples waterworks contract of the Banque Italio Suisse, the construction of the Rio Grande Slip Dock and the Tacuhy Navigation, the building of Kelly's sugar houses in Cuba and the iron piers of Ambriz, Fernan Vas, Old Calabar and the Senegal River; and the iron stations of the Guatemala and Costa Rica Railways. They also provided the machinery equipment of Robb's Sugar Estate, Cudgeon, New South Wales, and of Quintin Hogg's Plantations in British Guiana. Walter Carl B. was elected a member of the Institution of Naval Architects, and from time to time contributed to its meetings papers on the commercial economy of merchant steamers. Died at Helgoland, 16 July 1909."

Walter Carl Bergius and Agnes Catherine Walker Teacher were to have five children. Their eldest son, William Manera, as we will see, joined Wm Teacher & Sons. The next eldest, Walter, followed his father into marine engineering and started the Bergius Launch and Engine Company, manufacturers of the well-known Kelvin marine engines.

Together, the Teacher and Bergius families would build on William's dream and, through them, expansion on a grand scale was to take place.

ESTD · Wᴹ TEACHER & SONS · GLASGOW · 1830

CHAPTER TWO

MORE WHISKY SHOPS

William Teacher Senior was a true product of his age. His company started to grow at the beginning of Victoria's reign. Queen Victoria and her young husband Prince Albert, who often visited Scotland, were to rekindle interest in all things Scottish in England. Sir Walter Scott's novels were still popular and suddenly anyone who was anyone wanted to have their own tartan, kilts, sporrans and, of course, whisky. Queen Victoria and her husband embodied the country's thirst for knowledge, innovation, power, overseas supremacy and an all-consuming interest in what was right.

William Senior had all these qualities and more; driven, uncompromising, yet loved by his family and staff, he was to become a leading pillar of the local community. The hallmark of Teacher's, family, company and brand has always been one of not being afraid to be different, standing out from the crowd, yet at the same time not changing for change's sake.

The early 1830s were exhilarating times for a young man like William Teacher Senior who, as a member of the Unitarian Church and a reformer, was interested in the working conditions of his fellow men. In 1833 the Act of Emancipation was passed, which freed all slaves in British Territories.

From 1836, when the second shop opened in Cheapside, the company grew slowly. The Cheapside shop was just around the corner from Piccadilly, and William Senior secured a licence to sell whiskies in bottles. At that time whisky was only sold for consumption off the premises. New premises opened in 1837 at 8 Warroch Street and in 1841 at 13 McAlpine Street.

His family grew quicker, and the ratio of children to shops was about 2 to 1. The Glasgow Post Office Directories show the company as William Teacher, Grocer and Spirit Dealer for the most part, but by 1841 is listed as Wine and Spirit Merchant. The entry changes again in 1851 to William Teacher, Wholesale Wine and Spirit Merchant, 347 Argyle Street, Office 19 Maxwell Street. By the 1850s separate entries also appear for House, (his own home) and in 1864, 17 St Enoch Square (the new business headquarters).

The shop records in the Teacher archives start from 1856, but there are quite a few letters and other documents relating to the early years. For example, the letter dated 25 February 1837 (see opposite) shows an order for gin, brandy and whiskey currently in Bond written in William Teacher Senior's own hand.

The word "whiskey" is now mainly associated with Irish and American whiskies, but throughout the 19th century this spelling was commonly used in Scotland as well. The change appears to have come about at the beginning of the 20th century, although the Royal Commission on Whisky of 1908 still used "whiskey" in its findings.

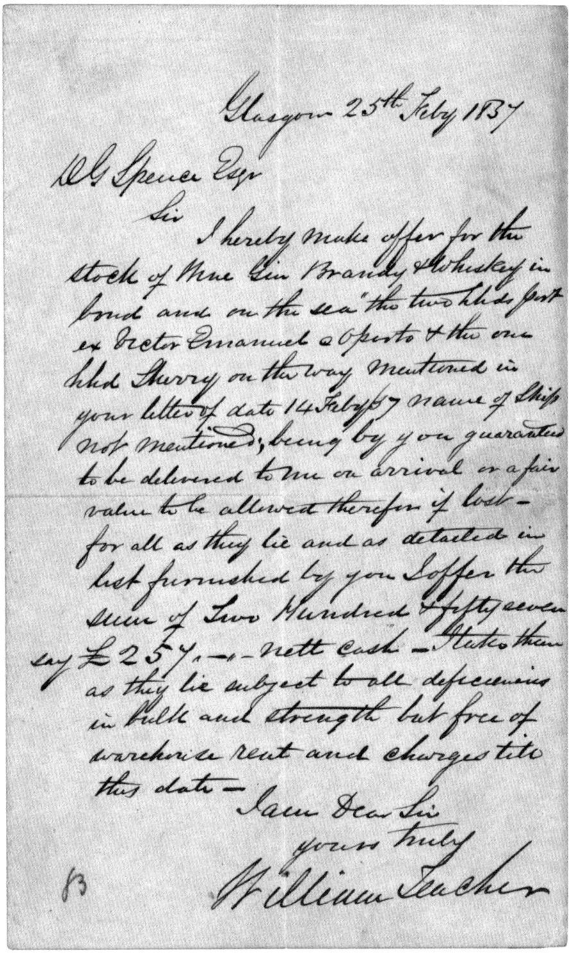

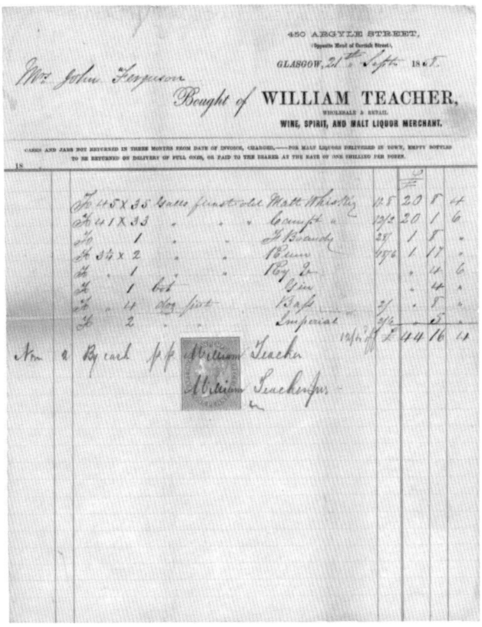

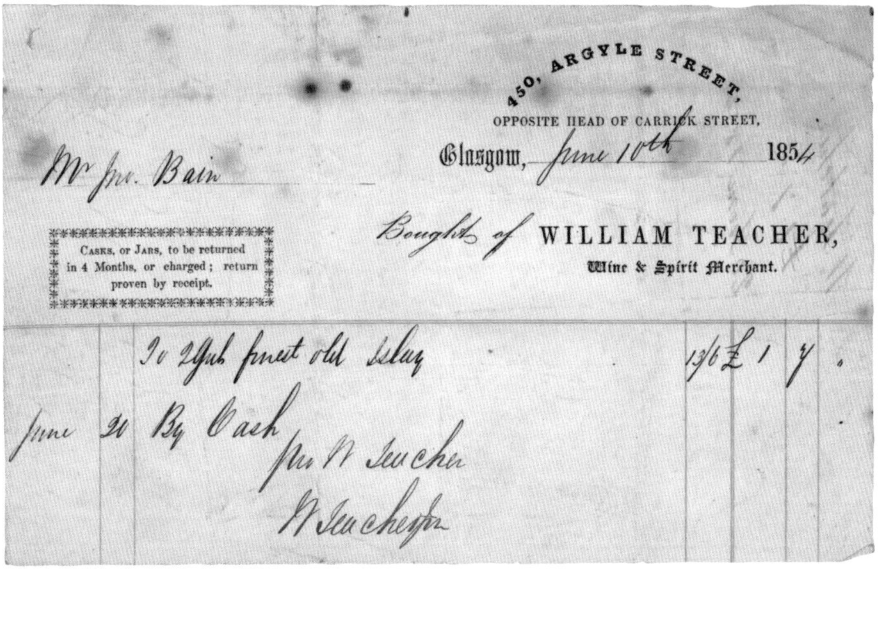

ADVERTISING

It is surprising how many newspapers were available to William for advertising purposes during those early years. Glasgow was home to the first Scottish newspaper, the *Glasgow Courant*, which came out in 1715 on Tuesdays, Thursdays and Saturdays in a small quarto format. The *Glasgow Courant* was to last for only 67 issues and closed in May 1716. Many newspapers were hampered by the imposition of Stamp Duty on daily newspapers.

In 1830, William Senior would have been able to buy *The Glasgow Journal* started in 1741, and the most successful of the early newspapers. This continued publishing until 1845 when it was purchased by the *Glasgow Chronicle*, itself launched in 1811 as a Liberal Whig voice, but ceased publication in 1857. The *Glasgow Chronicle* had been launched to offer a different editorial slant to the Tory (Conservative) inclined *The Glasgow Courier*, which started in 1791 and continued, although its fortunes declined considerably in the latter years, until 1866.

One newspaper which would have appealed to William Senior was the *Glasgow Free Press* set up in 1832, but unfortunately it had closed by 1835. There were a variety of other titles with the word "Reformer" included, which were all published by Peter Mackenzie, a Glasgow lawyer and political writer. His *Glasgow Reformer* was the most popular with a circulation of about 2,000, but closed in 1864. Mackenzie's aim was to "ferret out and expose frauds, impositions and abuses of all kinds." Another publication with a different approach was *The Scottish Guardian*, which was the voice of the Free Church from 1832–61.

The Glasgow Herald (1729–1845) was relaunched in January 1837 as *The Advertiser* and a rival to the *Glasgow Journal*. *The Advertiser*'s offices were in Gibson's Wynd, near Glasgow Cross. At first the newspaper was only published weekly, but after 1793 it appeared every Monday and Friday. *The Advertiser* changed its name to *The Glasgow Herald and Advertiser* in 1802, and finally, in 1834, to *The Glasgow Herald*. The article previously mentioned about the launch of the *Comet* steamship illustrates that this newspaper was a key source of local and national news.

Two other newspapers are worthy of mention, although not available to William Senior when he started in 1830. One is *The North British Daily Mail* (1847) a radical penny daily, which also featured trade-union and local activities. In 1901 it was sold to Lord Northcliffe and today is still available as the *Daily Record*. The other is the *Evening Times* (1876), which had the largest circulation for an evening paper and is still a leading voice on key issues. Advertisements would probably have simply listed the shops, the range of products available and shop opening hours.

TIPSY RULES

The growth of the wholesale side was slow as William Senior showed a distinct lack of enthusiasm for travelling outside Glasgow for business and the consequent necessity of having to give customers credit and deal with commercial travellers and "outsiders".

An important date for whisky distillers and retailers was 1830, as Aeneas Coffey patented his continuous still that year – this could produce over 910 litres (200 gallons) of clean grain spirit in only an hour.

In 1853, the Licensing (Scotland) Act was passed, or as it was more commonly described at the time, the Forbes Mackenzie Act. The Act was passed to bring grocers' shops under the licensing laws, as many of them were selling alcoholic drinks alongside food without requiring a licence. Under the Act grocers' shops could sell alcoholic drinks and food but should not be operated as a public house, inn or hotel. The Act created two types of licence to sell alcoholic drinks. One was for the sale of alcohol on the premises and the other for alcohol to be consumed off the premises – off-licences.

William Junior was granted a licence to sell whisky on the premises at 450 Argyle Street, the company's head office, on 6 May 1856 when he was just 19. Records show that applications for licences for this address were also made in 1852 and 1854, but these were refused.

To preserve anonymity the shops were given code letters. Notes in a file compiled by Walter Andrew Bergius in 1942 help place several shops. For example "K" was at 134 New City Road, "L" was clearly on a corner at 30/34 Stirling Road and 1 Barony Street, "I" at 144 St George's Road and "C" at 57 Clydeferry Street. Some of the roads have gone forever with the construction of new offices and warehouses and the building of the Glasgow Ring Road.

Walter Bergius writes, *"K E L G I H were quite out in the country with fields nearby. Anderston, in particular, containing C F and H was quite a separate village with green fields all round. The first Teacher shop was in Piccadilly Street, Anderston."*

Anyone driving from Glasgow to Anderston today could be forgiven for thinking that Walter Bergius was not telling the truth, as the City has all but taken over the countryside. In a car the journey is less than ten minutes (traffic permitting) from the city centre. But a glimpse of the countryside around the old area of Anderston does still exist. Drive along Argyle Street from Glasgow Centre and look to your right and you will see Kelvingrove Park, a large, green, open space, although I have yet to see cows and sheep grazing on the grass.

The shop drawings book of 1856–66 lists sales of different types of whisky, beers and other drinks. On 1 January 1857 sales were £56 17s., some £50 more than an average day,

Teacher's first paper bottle label probably dates from the 1860s. Shown here with William Teacher's accounting primer dated 1836.

Teacher's First Dram Shop 1856 in Argyle Street photographed in 1946.

obviously celebrating Hogmanay. By 1863 the dram shops were selling a wider range of alcoholic drinks.

Whisky is shown separately by cost, varying according to age or quality as well as Campbeltown, Grain or Malt and Dublin for Irish. Gin, Port, Sherry, Claret and Brandy Vignier, Brandy Martell and Brandy J. Hine, Beer and Porter are also listed. During this period off-licence sales increased including bulk whisky deliveries to other retailers, local restaurants and boarding houses. In the 1856–66 shop drawings book there is a reference to selling Port and "H.C." to John Smith of Garrick Street in 1863. On 8 February 1864 Mr Clew David of Burn Park Road, Partick, bought 2.8 H.C. @ 17s. 6d. per gallon.

The references to H.C. have provoked some additional research, as previous histories stated that the Highland Cream brand wasn't launched until 1870. From 1830 there was a consistent supply of grain whiskies, as well as single malts from all over Scotland. Whisky merchants, such as William Teacher, would have created their own signature blends. The official story is that blenders were only legally allowed to mix single malts and grain whiskies after the Blending Act was passed in 1865. It appears, however, that the Blending

1871 Renewal of
licence first issued in
1847 for 13 McAlpine
Street shop.

Scotland, No. 338.

Publican's Retail Spirit, Wine and Beer, Cyder and Perry Licence.

No. 423   No. 21

WE, whose Names are hereunto subscribed and Seals set, being the COLLECTOR OF EXCISE OF *Glasgow*

COLLECTION,* and the Supervisor of Excise of *Glasgow 2nd* District, within the said Collection, by virtue of the Authority to us given by the COMMISSIONERS OF INLAND REVENUE, and in pursuance of the Statutes in this behalf made, DO hereby license and empower *William Teacher* residing in a House known by the Sign of in the Parish of *Glasgow* in the County of *Lanark* and within the said Collection, (and duly authorized by the Justices of the Peace to keep a ~~Common Inn, Ale House, or Victualling House, [or]~~ a Public House or Premises for the sale therein of Spirits, Wine, &c., [or] of Porter, Ale, Beer, Cyder or Perry) to exercise or carry on the Trade and Business of a RETAILER OF SPIRITS, and FOREIGN WINE (having hereby license for Retailing Beer and Spirits) and TO SELL BEER, CYDER, OR PERRY, BY RETAIL,† at‡ *13 McAlpine Street* (as described by the Entry of the said Trader, dated *1st* Day of *February* 184*7* for carrying on therein the said Trade or Business, and as only one separate and distinct set of Premises, all adjoining or contiguous to each other, and situate in one Place, and held together for the same Trade or Business,) but nowhere else, from the Day of the Date hereof until the term of Whitsunday next ensuing, the said House at the Time of taking out this Licence, together with the Offices, Courts, Yards, and Gardens therewith occupied,§ being Rated, Rented, or Valued at a Rent or Annual Value of *16* Pounds per Annum or upwards, and under *20* Pounds, and he having paid the undermentioned Sum for this Licence to the said Collector of Excise.

Beer........£ *5-5-0*
Spirits *2-4-1*
Foreign Wine.

Dated this *16th* Day of *May* in the Year of our Lord 186*1*

Jno Callum, Collector

Wm Stewart Supervisor

N.B. The Continuance of this Licence depends upon the Continuance of the Magistrates' Authority upon which it is founded.

Renewal of Licence.

Every Person intending to continue the Trade or Business for which a Licence has been granted, is to give Notice of his Intention to the Collector or Supervisor at least Twenty-one Days before the expiration of his current Licence. If such Notice be so given, the new Licence must bear Date from the Expiration of his current Licence. If such Notice be not so given, the Licence must bear Date from the Day of the Trader's Application for it, and the Trader will be in the meanwhile unlicensed.

Penalty for exercising the above Trade without taking out or renewing Licence at the proper Time, £50.

Act was simply catching up with commercial reality. From the purchase ledgers in the archives, we can safely assume that William created his own blends using a wide range of whiskies from the very beginning. It is not inconceivable that by 1863 he had christened one of them H.C., or Highland Cream.

Some references to family purchases make strange reading. In 1865 William Teacher Junior bought a bottle of Port Wine and a Bottle of Claret, normal enough, but in 1866 William Teacher Senior bought "Hens meat" for £1 10s. and "3 Halfmutchkins" for £3. A Mutchkin was an old Scots measure, which was clearly still in use even though weights and measures had officially been brought into line with the English after the Act of Union in 1707. A Mutchkin was equivalent to 3 gills. An English gill is 5 fluid oz (about 150ml). I am not sure what the Hen's meat (presumably chicken?) refers to, although a Scots pint, which was equivalent to 4 Mutchkins, was also called a Tappit Hen.

William Senior had very clear ideas on how the shops should be run and they had none of the conviviality of today's public houses. Customers were not encouraged to while away the evening leaning on the counter drinking whisky. Music and skimpily clad ladies proffering drinks and cigars were certainly not the order of the day. Customers usually ordered a dram, which was served in a thick glass, paid for it and, once the glass was empty, left. Treating or buying a round was not allowed.

Agnes McDonald Teacher, William Senior's granddaughter, described this when telling her story to her niece Betty:

> *"My grandfather was a very upright man, a pioneer as Lindsay Wilson says in various causes, among others the Temperance Movement and Cancer. He and his sons were congratulated on being temperance reformers (no 'treating' was allowed in their shops i.e. one calling a round, then the next and so on) by the then Magistrates. He replied 'We are temperance reformers'. Auntie Aggie coming round in a ship from London was told by the Captain that as a young man he and five others went into one of Teacher's places and called for a drink, then a second, only to be told that no 'treating' was allowed. He said 'We were so surprised at any man only selling six drinks when he might have supplied 36, that they did not go elsewhere to continue'."*

Anyone who had over imbibed knew better than to go into a Teacher's shop and ask for a dram, for William Senior made it clear that anyone in a befuddled state should be refused. He also didn't allow smoking on the premises. It is ironic that 140 years later restrictions are being reintroduced to stop smoking in public places. William Teacher Senior would be surprised if he walked into an inn today by the array of drinks on offer and the relaxing atmosphere with food and places for children to play, but he would definitely say to himself, "I knew smoking was a bad thing to encourage!"

Teacher's Dram Shop Interior.

The rules William Senior put in place continued, as evidenced by the following extracts. In his book *Reminiscences*, William Bergius describes visiting the shops after the death of his uncle Adam on 31 March 1898.

"*Public house hours were from 8 a.m. till 11 p.m., but our shops closed (except on Saturdays) at 10.30. C, E, F, L, S were drinking shops, and D, I , K, M, O, although having full public house licences, did not allow drinking, but had a good carrying out or family trade.*

"*All our shopmen were Highlanders. At that time there was a steady influx from the North and West of Scotland to the city, and Teacher's employment was so well known that we always had a list of good men waiting for a start.*

"*The smaller shops had two men each. I think L had four, and F three, and hours were arranged so as to allow of the full staff being on duty for certain hours during which bottling was done.*

"*Serving customers took a minimum of time. A glass of whisky simply meant 3d on the counter, and a bottle was 2s. or 2s. 6d, according to quality. There was no wrapping up unless specially asked for by, e.g. old ladies. That was the business – customers were in*

and out of the shop in one minute. Little beer was sold, and whisky was always drunk neat. 'No Smoking' was absolutely enforced in the shops."

Dram Shop Rules issued to shop managers in May 1958 cover all aspects of running a dram shop, including opening and working hours, cash management, dealing with counterfeit coins, handling of beer, stocktaking, shop cleaning and how to get hold of the local police:

> *"Tipsy Persons: Never serve any person who is in the slightest degree under the influence of liquor, either for consumption on the premises, or for carrying out. If you are in any doubt as to his condition, not being quite sure if he really is under the influence of liquor you are to be on the safe side and refuse him. If a tipsy person forms one of a party, although the others may be perfectly sober, all are to be refused.*

> *"'Tipsys' Refusals and Police Visits: The book containing Tipsy refusals, Police Visits and the Children's Refusals is to be kept with the greatest care, and entries are to be made as soon as possible after refusal or Police Visit."*

THE TEMPERANCE MOVEMENT AND THE MOVE TO ST ENOCH SQUARE

In 1832 just after William Senior started working in the liquor trade, Joseph Livesey and seven working men living in Preston, England, signed a pledge that they would never again drink alcohol. In 1835 the British Association for the Promotion of Temperance was formed. The first members pledged not to drink spirits and they continued to drink wine and beer. By the 1840s societies started promoting teetotalism, which meant not just abstaining from drinking alcohol but also serving it to others.

The artist, George Cruickshank, whose own father (Isaac) had died of alcoholic poisoning, produced a series of illustrated books designed to persuade people to join the Temperance Movement. Members of the Quakers and Salvation Army petitioned the House of Commons to pass legislation to restrict the sale of alcohol. Public houses were forced to close on Sundays and permission to open new ones was often refused.

With the Temperance Movement in the background, local authorities started exercising stricter controls. A company such as Wm Teacher & Sons with its rules about dealing with inebriate behaviour would have appealed to the licensing magistrates.

As the number of shops grew, and with them the range of goods offered, changes were also taking place outside. George Stephenson had built the first railway line in 1814 to haul

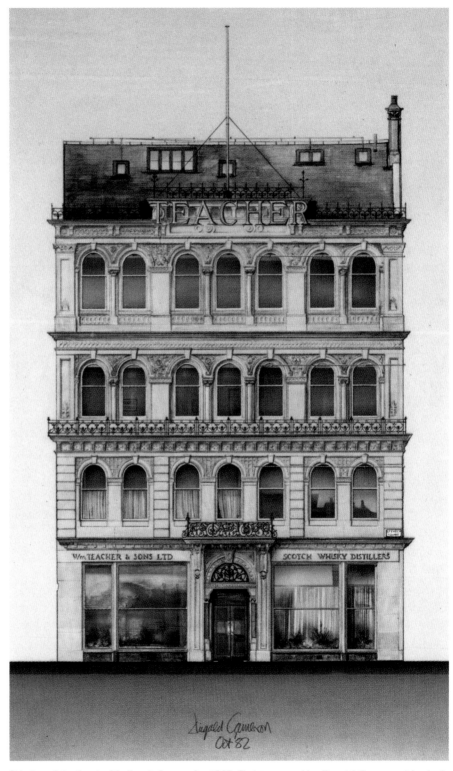

Painting of the front of St Enoch Square for 1983 Christmas card by Dugald Cameron, Head of Design, Glasgow School of Art.

coal. Since then great strides had been made and railway links built between Glasgow and the outlying areas, as well as the development of national lines. In 1842 Samuel Morse patented the electrical telegraph system developed by his assistant Alfred Vail. In 1860 the first radio was being developed and in 1866 the first transatlantic telegraph cable was laid. In 1869 work started on cutting the Suez Canal. The foundations were being made for the expansion of companies like Wm Teacher & Sons through improved transportation and communication links.

Another way the company promoted its business is mentioned in the list compiled by Walter Andrew Bergius in 1942. Under the entry for Shop M first licensed in 1873 Walter writes:

> *"There is a small advertising circular which states that whisky was 15s. per gallon and one bottle 1s. 3d. all duty paid. There is a small remark on this circular that the drawings was £14 per week."*

M was 282 Crown Street and 218 Cumberland Street, a property owned and part let to other tenants at the time of Walter's later memo regarding the proposed sale of the company's interests in the retail trade of 6 July 1960. But this is moving too fast.

Painting by Alex King of Glasgow Street in 1880 with Teacher's shopfront.

From this we see that the company was producing advertising circulars in the 1870s, but none of these have been found in the archives.

In 1864 the company had outgrown its premises in Argyle Street and moved into the centre of the city to 17 St Enoch Square. This was to be the headquarters until 1873 when the site was selected for the new St Enoch Railway Station. The firm then purchased a building on the other side of the Square, which they demolished and built as their new headquarters at Nos. 14, 16 and 18. To offset the huge total cost of £8,000 the building was occupied by a series of tenants. The last tenant, Messrs R. K. Gemmell, seed merchants, only vacated number 18 in 1965. Teacher's occupied the St Enoch Square premises from 1873 until 31 October 1991. Leaving St Enoch Square was a huge wrench for the remaining members of the Teacher family, as it had been the company's home for so long and contained such things as the Rennie MacIntosh Room. However, thanks to the efforts of the present member of the Bergius family, Bill, the façade and gilded metal lettering of 14–18 St Enoch Square are now listed and visitors to Glasgow can still see the "Teacher's" building for themselves.

Rennie MacIntosh Room photographed 11 November 1991.

WILLIAM ON HOLIDAY AND ADAM GOES TRAVELLING

One of the last Teacher's Dram Shops on the corner of Cumberland Street.

In 1868 William Senior travelled to the island of Malta and stayed in Sliema after an illness from nervous exhaustion. He sent several letters to the family and we can date one as it makes a reference to the fall of Madgala, a city in Abyssinia stormed by British troops under the command of Sir Robert Napier on 15 April 1868.

Lack of archival advertising material should not be seen as proof that the company did little to promote its products. This is far from the truth, as both William Junior and Adam were very active travelling the country and setting up a wholesale business with four representatives covering Scotland, and others were taken on to cover England and Wales. The fame of Wm Teacher & Sons and the company's whiskies and other products spread, and export sales started in the 1870s.

The 1870s were a busy time for the company, with William Junior and Adam taking a keen interest in its expansion. This is the first time that Teacher's Highland Cream is actively promoted, but as we have already seen it appears that a blend bearing the same name was marketed in 1863. Teacher's Highland Cream was registered in 1884 by Robert Hart, who had joined the company as an accounts clerk and was to become the first non-family partner in the business.

In September 1871 when he was 32, Adam set off on a trip to South America on board the *Tumuri*. He travelled with a friend, Ian Campbell, who was a naturalist. The only record of this trip is a journal, which covers the period 14 November 1871 to 6 February 1872. The log shows that the ship was loaded with a cargo of guano. As far as Campbell was concerned the aim of the voyage was to collect specimens, which were preserved in arsenic to stop rats eating them.

The voyage was eventful and many of the problems encountered during the voyage seem to have been caused by Captain MacDonald who was often drunk:

> *"25 December 1871: Splendid day, so we took advantage of it to explore north shore in hopes of sport. Got back to ship about 8 p.m. and found there had been a grand row as the men hadn't had a Christmas dinner and threatened they wouldn't work. Captain had battened them down under hatches and threatened them with starvation.*

> *"27 January 1872: Captain considerably the worse for liquor before breakfast. Got underway about 10 a.m. and were out and clear of the river by about 11 a.m. with a fine leading breeze for Port San Julian, 63 miles away. But to astonishment of all, orders given to shorten sail, and the day was frittered away.*

> *"29 January 1872: About 30 miles off our port. Got up within about six miles when ordered bout ship and stand out. Captain not the right thing. Wouldn't show face at table at any meal since leaving Santa Cruz. Men all grumbling about contradictory orders given."*

It isn't entirely clear whether Adam was intending to open up new markets or if he was just seeking adventure. It is true that the South American market opened up after a prolonged visit in Montevideo, Uruguay. There is very little reference to Teacher's whisky other than an entry on 31 December 1871: *"Exchanged one dozen bottles of Teacher's whisky for two skins of swan's down, a lion's skin, and some guanaco robes traded by the settlers."* Adam travelled with a revolver, a two-foot long jungle knife, a breech-loading Snider rifle and a double-barrelled shotgun – clearly he was taking no chances.

Edward Chisnall in his book *The Spirit of Glasgow* refers to the Teacher family, and Adam in particular:

> *"In the Teacher family, life and energy are in the blood as surely as there is strength and spirit in glass of the same name. Direct and true though they may be not one of them was ever quite as bold, eccentric, hard-hearted, wild, astute … Adjectives pale before the reality of Adam Teacher, the most colourful character of the entire family."*

He further describes him as "a buccaneer" and, looking through his journals and charting his business life, this is a pretty accurate description of someone who chose to be different. Adam was definitely following in his father's footsteps.

DEATH OF "OLD THOROUGH" AND HIS SON

On 27 December 1876, William Teacher Senior died. Although he had been slowing down a little, and seemed a little out of tune with the hurly-burly of business, no-one could have foreseen his death, as he was described as being as full of life and vitality as ever. The obituary in the *Scottish Standard* of 6 January 1877 was a fulsome one, giving an idea of the social standing of "Old Thorough" as well as the company he had founded. It also mentions what he looked like. Readers will recall that in the first chapter his great granddaughter described him as a "red-haired callant". By the time of his death he was described as having "long golden locks only just tempered with silver". The obituary also says *"His death was, we may say, unexpected by his friends, as he had all the appearance of a man who might live to a great age, being tall and active and of spare make …"*

William Senior burst a blood vessel and suffered a stroke after moving a heavy clock from the wall of his house: *"This his man-servant wanted to do – and being an able-bodied man was fully capable of doing – but Mr Teacher, with the energy and activity that always characterised him, resolved to do it himself, telling his servant that it was too heavy for him."* William died several days afterwards.

> *"Wherever Mr Teacher's name is known, and it is a household word in Scotland, his travellers girdling the length and breadth of the land, there will his death be deplored … Mr Teacher … was a self-made man, being originally, we believe, an operative cotton spinner. With the object of improving his position he left the Factory when young, and embarked in the Spirit Trade at a time, too, when there were not the same vexatious obstacles in the way of an entrance as there are now. Success attended his efforts, and he was enabled to gradually increase the number of his shops, until by himself and by his sons, he held more shops in Glasgow, we believe, than any other firm connected with the Trade."*

Most of William Senior's estate was tied up in the business and this meant that the partnership had to find the necessary financial resources to pay all his beneficiaries. This lack of separation between personal and business assets was to prove a continuing burden to successive generations and it wasn't until the 1920s, when a limited company was formed, that the situation could be finally resolved.

The first export order left the UK in 1878, destined for Messrs John Reid & Co Ltd of New Zealand. They became agents for Teachers in Auckland only. Over the next few years export markets gradually increased, with relationships being established in countries such as Norway, Italy, Holland, the West Indies, Australia and Thailand.

In her memoirs Agnes McDonald Teacher talks about her father William Teacher Junior: *"William Teacher Junior, son of William Teacher and Agnes McDonald, married Elizabeth*

Ann Curtis, (born in Barnstaple, Devon and came to Greenock with her parents and family when she was around 10 years old). They had five children. One of these children, William Curtis Teacher, was to go into the family business and another was, of course, Agnes McDonald Teacher, the author of these memoirs.

> *"He, my father, was a tall strong young man and Uncle Charlie once told me they were the best-matched pair he ever knew; [Uncle Charlie assumed to be William Senior's son, Charles Teacher, who became a doctor.] they often went fishing together. Unfortunately, when fishing up North by himself and very bad weather coming on, he caught a chill and developed a serious ailment. He was ordered abroad and spent two winters in Algiers, then Malta, where he died in his 42nd or 43rd year – a terrible grief to my mother."*

There is a letter on file from William Junior to his brother Adam from the Hotel du Nil, in Cairo dated 18 November 1879:

> *"My dear Adam, I hope this will reach you safely and find you in good health and not over-worried with the cares of the business. We had an unlucky journey from the very beginning. Commenced by losing the tide by 10 minutes and had to be all day in dock, not getting out till Monday 9 p.m. Crept down the Mersey like a snail, fog whistle going all the time. Next day was calm but with intensely cold east wind, in the evening it came on to blow, and we … [writing sadly indecipherable here] … which lasted us until within a few miles of Gibraltar. I got a very bad fall the first stormy day trying to avoid a sea coming on board, I slipped and was thrown right into the scuppers shaking me up terribly, bruising my ribs and pulling the muscles of my shoulder."*

His letter continues to talk about dining in Algiers which made him and his companions ill for three days:

> *"I got as thin as a rush for want of food … The run to here took seven hours, over a flat swampy line of country, yet the dust was simply infernal – it got into ones eyes, ears, nose, hair and clothes, and no amount of fluid would keep your day moist – 'choking' was Lizzie's continual cry."*

This hardly seems the ideal holiday for someone who was trying to gain strength by travelling to the sun.

On 12 April 1880, William Teacher Junior died, leaving Adam in sole charge. In 1880 Adam took his 17-year old nephew, William Curtis Teacher, into the business as an office boy. He was to become a partner in 1893.

Advertisement in "Scotland's Industrial Souvenir" publication for 1901 Exhibition.

External view of Teacher's London Offices at 60 Holborn Viaduct. People gather waiting for a parade to go by – believed to be celebrating Edward VII's Coronation 9 August 1902.

ESTD 1830

W^M TEACHER & SONS

GLASGOW

CHAPTER THREE

EXPANSION, EXPORTS AND A NEW DISTILLERY

The company was now in the hands of a young vibrant team: Adam Teacher, now 41; his young nephew William Curtis Teacher, not yet 17 years old; with the support of Robert Hart.

The private journals for 1882 show the company's turnover for 1881–82 as £101,843 0s. 7d. with an income of £6,747 12s. 2d. from the London office. The latter was set up in 1876 by William B. McKean, who had previously worked as a travelling salesman for a company known as Allsopps. Adam Teacher met William McKean on a train journey and offered him a job there and then. The Manchester office was then set up in 1886 by James Lightbody, who worked as a bookkeeper in Glasgow.

In 1887 Arthur Barnard published *The Whisky Distilleries of the UK*, at the back of which are various advertisements. One for *Harper's Weekly Gazette* has a facsimile front page dated 23 October 1886 featuring, "Wm Teacher & Sons, Glasgow; and 26 Philpot Lane, London EC. Our Australian Bonded Whisky will also be known under the same title with the additional Australian label."

Australian Bonded is another example of Teacher's innovation and their aim to produce a superior product by adding value. By this time distillers and wine and spirit merchants understood the merits of maturing whisky for some time in oak casks, but the length of time was usually quite short. All vessels travelling from the Clyde to overseas needed ballast certainly for the return journey. Ballast is used to stabilize a vessel, especially one that is not carrying cargo. Teacher's used the idea of transporting barrels of whisky to Australia and then bringing them back to Scotland, as a way of maturing the spirit. Thus Teacher's Australian Bonded Whisky was born.

The first request to members of the public to enter a new competition is from *The Daily Graphic* of Monday 20 November 1893. It asks for "Any Artist, male or female, professional or amateur, to design a Coloured Show Tablet for Teacher's 'Australian Bonded' and 'Highland Cream'." The reward was 50 guineas (see page 58).

In 1893, another of Adam Bergius' nephews, William Manera Bergius, joined the company, albeit somewhat reluctantly. His book *Reminiscences*, published in 1938, records the following:

> *"When I found myself on Wednesday 3 August 1893 in my uncle Adam Teacher's office at 14 St Enoch Square I felt very 'out of place'. It was the middle of my summer holidays, and I had always thought I was going to be an engineer! And I hadn't even thought of leaving school yet."*

The *Bergius Family Tree* entry for William Bergius is as follows:

> "William Manera, born 30 September 1877, was educated at Hillhead Public School and Kelvinside Academy, Glasgow. In 1893 he started as office boy in Wm Teacher & Sons, and in 1898 on the death of his uncle Adam Teacher, became a partner along with his cousin Wm C. Teacher, and Robert Hart. Married 1 June 1909, to Agnes Hunter Bayne at Glasgow. In 1921, together with Wm C. Teacher, formed a private company, Wm Teacher & Sons Ltd. He was appointed Managing Director and developed the various fields of the business, particularly the export trade. Upon the

TEACHER'S WHISKIES.

THE

"HIGHLAND

CREAM."

AND

"AUSTRALIAN

BONDED."

REWARD 50 GUINEAS.

MESSRS. WILLIAM TEACHER & SONS desiring to obtain a highly artistic COLOURED SHOW TABLET for their celebrated "AUSTRALIAN BONDED" and "HIGHLAND CREAM" WHISKIES, offer the above prize of FIFTY GUINEAS to any Artist, male or female, professional or amateur, for the best design, the skeleton sketch given above, being the basis on which the work is to be executed. All persons in the show card trade are excluded from this competition, and professional artists or members of any Academy or Institution of Painters, if entering, and being adjudged the winner, shall forfeit to the second best designer, such being an amateur, TEN GUINEAS of the above prize.

The Judge to be appointed by the Principal of the Firm. The size is to be 36 inches in width by 30 inches in depth, including the frame.

All persons intending to enter for this Prize must send full name and address to 26, Philpot Lane, E.C., within one month of the appearance of this intimation. The designs are to be delivered at the firm's offices, as above, on or before 1st of February, 1894.

Competitors who are acquainted with the "Australian Bonded" and "Highland Cream" Whiskies will find that the knowledge of the article they are called upon to illustrate will materially help in the creation of the Picture.

683

death of Wm C. Teacher in 1929 he became the Chairman until the time of a flotation
of a holding company, Teacher (Distillers) Ltd, in 1949. Ultimately the business grew
into the largest Scotch Whisky Company outside the Combine. (Distillers Company
Limited) Died 4 October 1950."

The first export ledger in the Teacher's Archives dates from 1894–1914 and is written in a fine copperplate hand. References are also made elsewhere in 1893 to agencies in Bombay, Rangoon, Columbo and Calcutta. In the ledger there is an extensive list of destinations, including Port of Spain, Trinidad, Paris, Rome, Bayonne, Boulogne-sur-Mer, Riga and Ostend. The company continued to develop export markets, including France which turned to whisky as a substitute to cognac, unavailable following the decimation of the French vineyards by the Phylloxera aphid, which had arrived from America in 1863. Robert Hart started travelling abroad and in 1894 he visited Scandinavia and secured the first Norwegian order for Teacher's from Robert Prizelius and Co. They continued representing Teacher's until the 1970s.

The 1894–1914 ledger also provides an insight into the type of advertising and promotional material produced by the company. For example, Dr A. Smyth & Co., at 18 rue de la Chausée d'Antin, Paris, on 27 February 1896 received samples and also three small mirrors, 12 transparencies, one iron, 100 leaflets, 100 LVG, 1 Opal, 1 Jeloleum, 1 Band. On further research Opals, Irons and Jeloleums are showcards but no examples remain in the Teacher archives. The LVG reference is to an article which appeared about Teacher's in the *Licensed Victuallers' Gazette* of 1896.

Some entries in the ledgers relate to other purchases. In 1895 the vessel Norse King enters the books as "Steam Yacht a/c for sums paid on 70 ordinary and 30 preference shares of £10 each – at £6 per share." It is not clear why this boat was purchased and indeed Teacher's sold the *Norse King* in 1898 to Dr Henry Lunn. He renamed the steam yacht *Argonaut* which became the first package-tour holiday ship run by Lunn's Tours, later Lunn Poly. *Lunn's steamer*, as she was known, made her first cruise in 1898. The *Argonaut* finally sank in 1908 in Rye Bay, Sussex.

References to foreign and home advertising also start to appear in the Teacher's company Private Journals. For example, on 31 January 1897 the totals are shown for Foreign Advertising as £663 9s. 1d. and Home Advertising as £456 4s. 2d. At the same time Teacher's have interests in the Convalmore Distillery, the Bristol Hotel and Blackpool Winter Gardens.

The evolution of the distillery in Dufftown has a chequered career, as documented by *The Scotch Industry Record* by H. Charles Craig, 1994:

"Convalmore-Glenlivet Distillery Co. Ltd built the distillery in Dufftown, Banffshire
in 1894 … Purchased from liquidator by W. P. Lowrie & Co Ltd for £6,000 plus stock

at 2s. 6d. per gallon in March 1905 who were from 1906 controlled by James Buchanan
& Co. Ltd. Rebuilt 1909–10 when experiments were made with continuous distillation
of malt spirit. Passed to the DCL in 1925 and transferred to SMD 1930. Extended from
two to four stills 1964. Licensed to W. P. Lowrie & Co. Ltd. Closed 1985 and site sold to
Wm Grant & Sons 1990."

Teacher's first colour advertisement with traditional cork stopper c1900

Ever since William Senior had started selling whisky in 1830, the company had been totally dependent on outside distilleries for its supply. Adam Teacher believed that the company should build its own distillery in order to exercise more control on the quality of the finished product, and fulfil anticipated demand. In 1895 the partners purchased land near Kennethmont in Aberdeenshire. Building did not start until 1897 and the distillery took over a year to complete. Adam was, however, never to see his dream finished, as he died on 31 December 1898. The new distillery was named Ardmore and to this day provides a distinctive single malt, which is an important part of Teacher's Highland Cream.

ADAM'S DEATH AND DEBT AND DISASTER

Once more the death of a senior partner, or in this case the only real partner, was to throw the business into chaos. At his death Adam Teacher's personal estate was worth around half-a-million pounds and a large percentage of this was tied up in the company.

As William Manera recorded:

> *"At Adam Teacher's death in 1898 we were faced with an impossible task. Adam Teacher was the sole proprietor of the business apart from very small shares held by Mr Teacher and Mr Hart, and the new firm accordingly owed his Trustees all the capital involved, some £360,000 with interest at 4 per cent, the total to be paid out in ten years … We found ourselves with Ardmore Distillery half built, and a good block of shares in the Ardgowan Distillery Co., Greenock, also half built. None of us knew anything about distilling. Adam Teacher's friend, the late Duncan MacCullum of Glendronach, gave him James Innes to supervise the building of Ardmore Distillery and he was brewer until his death in 1923.*

> *"Joseph T. Townsend, another of Adam Teacher's friends, had got us into the formation of the Ardgowan Distillery Co., and what Joseph didn't know about distilling wasn't worth knowing. I got much valuable information from him in the course of the years. He was proprietor of Scapa and our annual filling was 100 Butts at 2s. 10d., so, as his best customers, he was often about our office, and very pleased to give information."*

The Scotch Industry Record by H. Charles Craig, 1994, explains the history of the Ardowan Distillery: *"Ardgowan Distillery was a grain distillery built in 1896 and promoted by 'a group of blenders including Pattisons Ltd, John Robertson & Son Ltd, Dundee, William Teacher & Sons and John Walker & Sons. Taken over by the DCL 1907 and closed. Company liq. 1907–8'."* Up to July 2005, both Scapa and Glendronach distilleries along with Teacher's were part of Allied Domecq portfolio.

Adam Teacher never married and a clue to why he didn't may be in Agnes McDonald Teacher's (William Senior's granddaughter) notes: *"Uncle Adam had admired my mother very much before she married my father."* Whether he had more than a passing interest in Elizabeth Anne Curtis we will never know.

Agnes goes on to describe Adam:

> *"He was, I understand, a good living man. Uncle Adam and my father were great friends and used to go cruising in their small yacht, even across the Minch where once they were reported lost in a storm. In later life he travelled considerably. He also went salmon fishing and took grouse shootings up North. He was a reader, especially of*

James Innes, the first manager of Ardmore Distillery.

books on travel and biographies. He was a good friend to rising young artists and his collection of pictures was left to the Glasgow Art Galleries."

This important collection of pictures is still with Glasgow Art Galleries, although much of it hasn't been on display for a long time. *The Catalogue of the Teacher Bequest of Pictures* was printed by Robert Anderson, 142 West Nile Street, in 1905. The Introductory Note states:

"Mr Adam Teacher, of 8 Marlborough Terrace, Glasgow who died on 31 March 1898, under his deed of settlement bequeathed to the Corporation of Glasgow his collection of 'paintings, pictures, and curios'. The pictures, which in this generous and untrammelled manner became public property numbered 117, and a complete list of them will be found in the following pages. Mr Teacher's collection consisted wholly of modern works, many of them by artists yet living. And while they embrace representative works of some of the Continental schools, it will be seen that the major proportion of the works are by Scottish artists. Undoubtedly it is in this department that the Teacher Bequest is strong and significant, and it is a fortunate circumstance that adequate and typical works of numerous Scottish artists, hitherto unrepresented in the Corporation Collections, have in the way been added to the art treasures of the City."

Key artists, who represented the Scottish School, include Joseph Donovan Adam with a painting of *In Clover – Shore of a Highland Loch with Luxuriant Vegetation*. The catalogue states that, *"In 1871 he [Joseph Adam] took up his residence in Scotland, and quickly attained both popularity and success as a painter of Highland cattle, depicted amid hilly and moorland surroundings."*

There are also 16 paintings by Alexander Fraser who was one of the most eminent Scottish landscape painters. The catalogue continues:

"His first exhibited work at the Royal Scottish Academy was 'A Gypsy Girl in Prison' – but he soon gave up figure painting, and turned his attention entirely to landscapes. His best works, which were for the most part painted in the open air, are scenes in Surrey and Cadzow Forest and are distinguished for their purity, richness and vigour of colour and their fidelity to nature."

Adam's collection includes three of the Cadzow Forest, as well as other Scottish scenes.

Another featured artist is William Ewart Lockhart (1846–1900), best known for his painting, commissioned by Her Majesty Queen Victoria, of *The Jubilee Celebration in Westminster Abbey* which now hangs in the Royal Galleries, Windsor. Adam had four of his paintings, two of St. Andrew's, one entitled *Near the Hague* and the other *Palace of the Duke of Montpensier*.

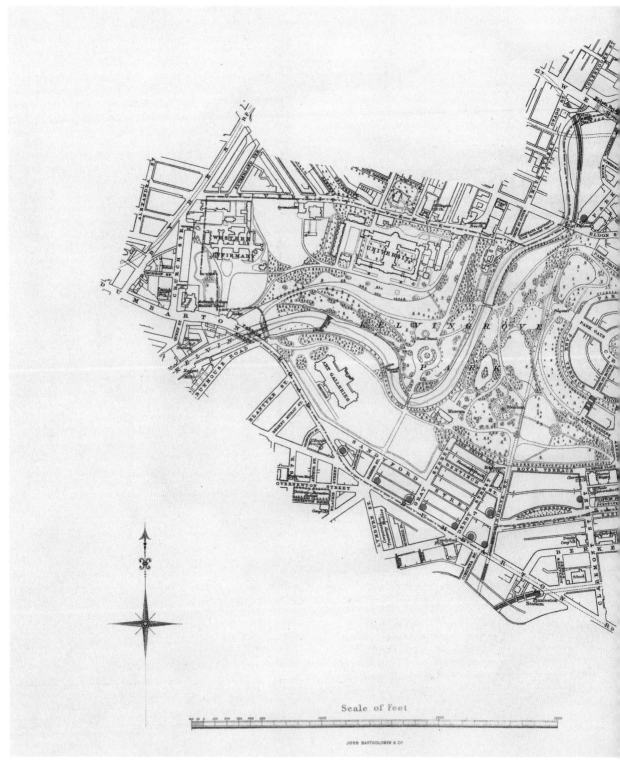

1902 Map of Glasgow showing licensed premises in Ward 15 Park. Teacher's had a shop at 144 St George's Road from 1873.

WARD 15

PARK.

NOTE:_____
PUBLIC HOUSES SHEWN THUS
LICENSED GROCERS ,,   ,,
HOTELS   ,,   ,,
PREMISES CLOSED SINCE MAY 1901

Adam left £50,000 to Glasgow Charities, subject to the authorities renewing licences on several shops, which were under negotiation at the time of his death. Unfortunately, some of them weren't renewed, and based on the value of the licences some £14,000 was deducted from the bequest.

1898 was also a catastrophic year for all whisky distillers, not just Wm Teacher & Sons, for a quite different reason. The prominent whisky blenders Walter and Robert Pattison's business collapsed. Pattisons were involved with Teacher's and others in Ardgowan Distillery. Pattisons was set up to meet the insatiable demand for Scotch. For while Teacher's was growing, so too was the rest of the industry. Production of whisky, both grain and malt, more than doubled. This was a period of huge whisky investment: not only was Teacher's building Ardmore, but new distilleries were springing up throughout Scotland. At the same time, sales around the world and across the border in England increased. But finally, production far exceeded demand and it soon became apparent that the Pattison brothers had created their vast empire on credit and fraudulent borrowing. The collapse of Pattisons was to have a significant effect on the industry – many other companies went into liquidation and investors in the whisky market withdrew their support.

W. H. Ross of the Distillers Company wrote in the *DCL Gazette* of April 1924:

> *"So large were their transactions and so wide their ramifications that they infused into the trade a reckless disregard of the most elementary rules of sound business. Encouraged by the ease with which financial assistance could be obtained from the Scotch banks of the day, investors and speculators of the worst kind were drawn into the vortex and vied with each other in their race for riches."*

The next years were difficult ones for Wm Teacher & Sons, trying to wrestle their way out of the debts incurred following family members' deaths. Export markets continued to grow and in 1900 destinations included Boston USA; Barcelona; Hamburg; Newhaven Connecticut USA; Singapore; La Paz Bolivia; Quito; and Mauritius. In 1900 Teacher's started producing a series of Calendars entitled "Heroes, Generations and Musicians". A shipment to Iceland on 19 February 1901 included "3HC electro blocks". Racing cards also became a recurring item, with deliveries to the Royal Natal Yacht Club in 1907.

The records also list the ships used, mostly Clan Line, including *Clan Graham*, launched in 1882, and *Clan Matheson*, in 1883, both built by Napier Shanks & Bell Yoker, *Clan McNab* in 1891 and *Clan Mackinnon*, again launched in 1891, were built by Alexander Stephen & Sons, Glasgow. Shipping had certainly come a long way from the maiden voyage of the *Comet* in 1812.

In 1906 Robert Hart died and his trustees were owed £60,000 by the company. In the end the trustees settled for £45,000. Then Lloyd George's budget of 1909 raised spirit duty from 11 shillings to 14s. 9d., which cut profits to the bone.

WILLIAM MANERA BERGIUS, INNOVATION AND RATIONING

When Agnes Catherine Walker Teacher married Walter Carl Bergius she chose someone who would inject academic engineering, innovation and analysis into the family. Their son, William Manera, brought all these skills and an enquiring mind when he joined the family firm to work with his uncle Adam in 1893.

Whisky at the time was supplied in bottles, which were closed with a wine cork, which tapered from top to bottom. All too often the cork broke in the bottle, or was damaged so it could not be replaced – just in case you did not want to finish the whisky that night!

William Manera invented a new closure in 1913, a cork with a rim at the top, which tapered the other way, that is from bottom to top. This could easily be removed by twisting it out of the bottle, as only the bottom of the cork made a seal. In *A Family of Spirit*, Geoffrey Cousins writes that Adam Bergius, William Manera's youngest son, said of his father that *"the idea of gradually applied power came to him as he watched a steam locomotive 'back-up' a long line of coal trucks so that it could, in the length of the slack in each coupling, get them moving one at a time until the whole train was in motion."*

This invention was to herald the launch of the company's biggest advertising and public-relations campaign to date. "The Self-Opening Bottle" was the caption and the device attracted a great deal of attention in the trade and national press. Anyone running a marketing department today would have been ecstatic at the results. There must have been a good copywriter in the company – perhaps William Manera himself? The press coverage, for the most part, uses the same phrases and follows the same theme – a great success in terms of marketing and getting the message across. Luckily for us, the original printing blocks for this campaign were discovered in a box in an old filling store at the Glendronach distillery. Teacher's were to lead the way with this device for 15 years.

the best horse trained in this country for a long time, and not only was the style in which he smashed up such a brilliant handicap horse as Long Set in the Coronation Cup convincing, but his expected Gold Cup victory at Ascot was gained with great ease. It is understood that Mr. Pilkington has had a tempting offer for the Prince, but the horse is not for sale.

THERE was plenty of excitement associated with Ascot this year, but form panned out well, and there were not nearly so many startling results as have been produced here in previous years. Long Set certainly stamped himself as the best handicap horse in training by winning the Royal Hunt Cup under an impost of 9 st. 1 lb., and the performance was enhanced by one of the beaten lot, Braxted, subsequently taking the Wokingham Stakes for Sir Thomas Dewar.

THE Irish three-year-old, Sleipner, was certainly set a severe task to carry 7 st. 11 lb. in the Royal Hunt Cup, but the colt still proved his smartness by showing very prominently for about six furlongs of the journey. Mr. Cogan had sent the horse over to Frank Hartigan to be trained for this engagement, and, if he failed here through inability to stay, there is still a fine chance left for him in the Stewards' Cup at Goodwood on the 29th inst. It will take something very smart to beat Sleipner here.

THERE was some difficulty in obtaining a satisfactory entry for the Liverpool Summer Cup this year, and the race had to be reopened. It has now closed with 21 subscribers, and quality is best represented by Bachelor's Hope, Maiden Erlegh, Long Set, Lomond, and Stedfast. These are a smart lot from which the winner should come, and I may say that if there was such good reason to support Maiden Erlegh in the Royal Hunt Cup he may be good enough to win. The distance should be just to the liking of Mr. Sol Joel's horse.

MAIDEN ERLEGH is, however, previously engaged in the London Cup, which is to be decided over the Alexandra Park course on the 5th inst. He is here weighted on the same mark as Bachelor's Hope, at 9 st. 1 lb., but, should the race be chosen for him, my readers would do well to follow the Hunt Cup failure here.

THE Ayr Summer Meeting is certainly a welcome arrangement to holiday-makers in the West of Scotland, and on 21st and 22nd July we should see an enormous concourse at this popular resort. The programme is on the usual attractive lines, and as the events already closed have obtained numerous entries we are promised a plentiful supply of runners.

As no weights are to hand at the time of writing, it is impossible to venture upon selections, but I note that Mr. Gilpin has a few entrants, and whatever is sent from this Newmarket stable will be worth looking after. Mr. J. B. Thorneycroft may also have a winner in Red Gate, as this is a much improved animal.   NORTHERN SPY.

A THIRD edition of "Vegetable Culture for Amateurs" (L. Upcott Gill, 1s. net) proves the efficiency and the public appreciation of this excellent practical handbook.

SWIMMING.

THE S.A.S.A. handbook contains all information concerning rules, ordinary competitions, championships, records, and guidance to officials and referees. It is such as every one connected with the sport will find a most serviceable pocket companion. Special features of this latest edition are :— world's records, international agreements, and international swimming Federation rules.

✤

THE long-distance championship will this year be swum off at Gourock. The race may be a little longer than last year's, but the change of the course from the other side of the Firth will not be any less convenient.

✤

ENTRIES close this month with Mr. W. A. Lawson, secretary of the Scottish centre of the Royal Life-Saving Society, for this

Mr. JOHN G. M'LAUCHLAN,
President, Western Counties Amateur Swimming Association.

session's championships. In the Scottish championship for the Waddell Shield, clothing has been dispensed with, and S.A.S.A. swimming costume substituted, for the water drill. The events are :—for the British National Shield, the British Ladies' Challenge Cup, the Darnell Challenge Cup, the Waddell Shield, the Scottish Ladies' Trophy, and Scottish Junior and Juvenile Trophies.

✤

THAT Paisley is the undoubted centre of water-polo in Scotland at the present time no one connected with the sport will deny, and it is only in the fitness of things that a member of the champion club of that town should now occupy the highest office in the western district governing association. More appropriate still, Mr. John G. M'Lauchlan, who has entered on his second year of office as president of the W.C.A.S.A., qualified for the responsible position which he now occupies by the assiduity he displayed in the interests of the game of which his clubmates have proved such adepts. Coming to the association as their delegate some ten years ago, he has, as convener of the water-polo committee for

a considerable period, earned surely, albeit by a less varied route than any of his predecessors, the unstinted confidence and highest appreciation of his colleagues at the District Board. Although devoted particularly to polo, he has proved himself, during his term of office, thoroughly alive to the great possibilities of every phase of the art of swimming.

✤

SINCE the institution, 13 years ago, of the Glasgow Corporation Shield race, which is virtually the public baths championship of Glasgow, the trophy has been won, except in 1905 and 1906, when the governing association was divided, by the South-Side and Glasgow Amateur clubs, and, but for that same split, it is more than probable that only one club would have been recorded as winners up to the present time. The chief reason for this unhealthy monopoly of an honour which was intended to stimulate enthusiasm in every district, but the contests for which have latterly been looked upon with apathy, has been, in my view, to a large extent, its restriction to the sprinting class of swimmers. This in Scotland has for many years been a grievance in all collective competitions, but, happily, a forward step has at last been made in the Glasgow shield race, and this year each member of the competing teams will have to swim 100 yards, instead of 50 as previously.
                                                    TRUDGEN.

CLEAR-WATER worm-fishing forms the subject of a thoroughly practical article with which Mr. W. J. Cummins, the well-known tackle-maker of Bishop Auckland, prefaces his latest price list of appliances for this form of angling sport. The whole pros and cons of the process are succinctly set forth in these few pages, and the July angler will do well to write for a copy of the brochure. "When I say worm-fishing," says Mr. Cummins, "I mean fishing in low, clear water, as any novice may capture trout when the waters are coloured. But to angle with the worm scientifically, the greatest care is required in casting ; the habits of the trout must be understood, all feeding places well known, and the finest tackle used if the angler would succeed."

IF you have not a corkscrew the fact does not matter if the bottle you seek to open is one of Teacher's "Highland Cream" Whisky. This firm has adopted a new, simple, and ingenious device, which consists of a metal cap over the cork perforated round the edge like a postage stamp, and all that is required in order to withdraw the cork is to give the top a turn either way. The excellence of the device is in keeping with the excellence of the contents which become available as a result of the operation. Our illustration gives an idea of the new invention.

"VANITY FAIR" CARTOON.

"You would be told, would you, the history of the *Vanity Fair* cartoon of Mr. Gant done years ago. There is no history attached to it that I know. A series of prominent sportsmen were being caricatured, and 'Spy' hit upon me. I had at that time established myself as the 'no-limit man' ; the novelty which I conceived had then taken hold of the people. The idea of my £50,000 being put up for the speculating public to run at gripped 'Spy' as it did everybody else. And so you see D. M. Gant (of 41 New Bond Street, London), here, there, and everywhere."—*Sporting Life.*

As early as 1914 Teacher's were sponsoring sport and in the archives there is a record of the Bowling Handicap, which was held on the green attached to the Swan Hotel in Woolfold. The cuttings from the licensed trade press, including *Harpers Weekly* and the *Licensed Victuallers' Gazette*, report that, *"The first prize, presented by Messrs William Teacher & Sons, Glasgow, consisting of a beautiful set of silver-mounted bowls and jack in a leather bag, was won by Mr A. Halliwell, defeating Mr S. W. Howarth in the final."*

The First World War (1914–18) meant that Wm Teacher & Sons sadly lost a family member, as William George Teacher was killed in Action in 1916. William Manera takes up the story during the Great War years:

> *"In 1915 we had to give up our Scotch Trade owing to the passing of the Immature Spirit Act, and for three years, from 1916–19, we ceased our bottling, there being insufficient labour available for work of this sort. Customers were supplied with HIGHLAND CREAM in bulk, and given labels and paper capsules. When we resumed after all the difficulties and disputes we had with our customers during those difficult times, there seemed comparatively little good will lost, and we, on our part, as a new policy, tried our very best to make our labelling and 'get-up' as perfect as we knew how."*

This all seems a little strange today, where so much care and effort is put on ensuring that bottles are properly labelled and sealed before they leave the bottling plant.

William Manera invented a rationing system using voucher cards, as the government restricted sales of alcohol during the First World War. The scheme was introduced on 3 December 1917. William wrote:

RATION TICKET.

Write your name and address on back of this card and on this envelope, and bring it back with your registration card any day next week.

Each customer can only register in one of our shops.

Any customer attempting to register in more than one shop, or more than once in the same shop, will be disqualified.

WM. TEACHER & SONS.

RATIONING SCHEME.

In response to your application, we have pleasure in advising having placed your name on our Customers' Register.

Ration Card for fortnight ending 15th December, 1917, is enclosed. This entitles you to receive 10 half-gills of Spirits, 5 gills, or one bottle during the period. A full section—containing the whole of our Trade Mark—must be left with the Shopman for each gill served, and a half section—containing half Trade Mark—for each half-gill. Sections must not be detached, but the whole card presented to Shopman.

The cards are not transferable, and are only available at the shop where application for registration was made. If transferred, card will be forfeited and name taken off our Register. Shopmen are authorised to ask for production of National Registration Card for proof of identity.

All further cards will be issued from shops in exchange for section marked " Exchange Card."

WM. TEACHER & SONS.

1st December, 1917.

VOUCHER CARD LOST.   **B**

Date,............................. Shop,.............

Exchange Card (Number),......................

" any day after (Date),"......................

Period Number,......................

Whether " On " or " Off,"......................

If number known for certain, and following Voucher Card not already issued, immediately withdraw it, and in its place put this Card.

COPIED FROM NATIONAL REGISTRATION CARD :

Name,......................

Whether Mr., Mrs., or Miss,......................

Address,......................

....

District,......................

" A " Copy returned (Date),......................

SEE INSTRUCTIONS ON OTHER SIDE.

7–F   EXCHANGE SECTION.   417

Card for another period issued in exchange for this section any day after 11th February, 1918, but not available after 6th April, 1918.

New Card will be issued in exchange whether or not use is made of Ration Tickets.

417

7 F   F 7

Detached sections are NOT accepted.
The whole card must be presented.

7 F   F 7

Only available Week ending 16th February, 1918.

7 F   F 7

Only available Week ending 16th February, 1918.

7 F   F 7

Only available Week ending 16th February, 1918.

7 F   F 7

Only available Week ending 16th February, 1918.

Registered Number.

Customers are respectfully requested to kindly note that number of each fresh Voucher Card received agrees with their Registered Number, which is printed above.

This envelope is also suitable for holding National Registration Card. If lost, customer should report immediately to shop, so that number can be stopped.

When envelope becomes worn or dirty, kindly present it, asking for a fresh one.

A simple promotional device Teacher's produced, which allowed customers to plot the progress of the 1914-1918 War.

"As the result of other Licensees running short of Spirits in the autumn of 1917, a constantly progressive demand was experienced which ultimately threatened to make the shops unmanageable owing to crowding. In addition, stocks were being diminished at a greater rate than it was possible, owing to restrictions upon clearances from Bond, to renew. It was concluded that closing down as soon as a certain quantity had been sold would not afford a satisfactory solution, as the knowledge that shops would be closed early would only lead to a scramble at opening time. Rationing was considered the best plan."

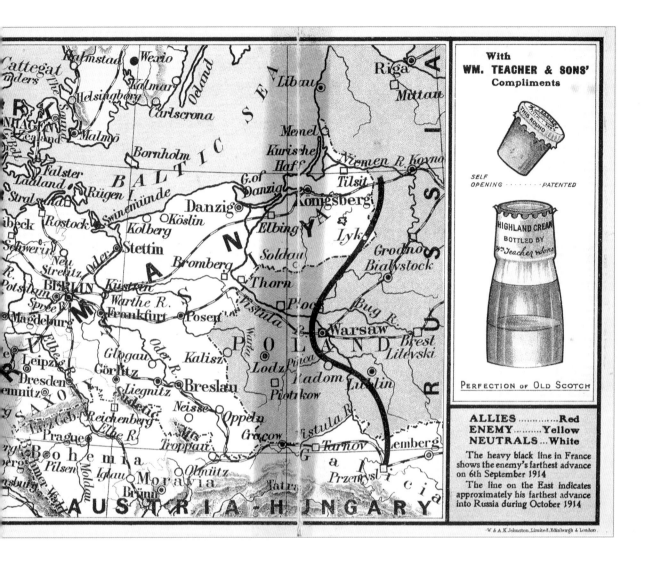

William described how people could apply for a voucher card, the value of each card, the setting up of registers in each shop so that the cards could be properly controlled and honoured. The system allowed for the consumption of spirits both "On" and "Off" the premises. The cards allowed customers a bottle every two weeks or five glasses a week. The cards were issued fortnightly and procedures were also set up for the reissue of lost voucher cards. Sailors and Soldiers wearing H.M. Uniforms were served without ration-card vouchers, but the allowance was restricted to 1 glass per day "On" or 1 gill per day "Off".

The Glasgow Herald on 19 December 1917 reported, *"… it is also giving great satisfaction to the customers for the reason that Messrs Teacher's have been able to continue selling at the old price, whereas the rest of the Trade have been forced to advance prices for the purpose of conserving stocks."* William himself recalled, *"When the meat-rationing regulations came into being shortly afterwards the cards and arrangements were practically identical with ours. We felt very proud of our good old shops."*

THE SEA, ARTISTIC COLLECTIONS AND CHARITABLE DONATIONS

There are several recurring threads which run through the lives of all members of the Bergius and Teacher families. The first is the sea, whether working on it as a sailor, or as a marine engineer or sailing for pleasure. Every generation had a boat of some kind and this still holds true today.

The second theme is an interest in the arts, and Adam Teacher's collection has already been described in the previous chapter. As the company grew Teacher's commissioned the artist Cecil Aldin to create promotional posters for them. Cecil Aldin was born on 28 February 1870 at Wellington Lodge, Slough. He was the son of Charles Aldin, a builder who with his father and brother William built over 400 houses in South Kensington, including some 200 of the large Italianate, stucco-fronted buildings that still survive today. When Cecil was one, the family moved to live in Durham Villas, now Phillimore Place in Kensington. Cecil started drawing and painting early on and some of his childhood pictures of horses and dogs survive. In time he was to become one of the most celebrated illustrators of his day, creating pictures for the *Illustrated London News* from 1892 until late in his life.

Together with other members of the thriving artistic movement in Chelsea who challenged the authority of the establishment, he formed the London Sketch Club in 1898. Apart from his drawings, Cecil was also well-known for a whole series of children's books including *The Happy Family* and featuring among others, *Hungry Peter – the Pig*, and *Humpty and Dumpty – the Rabbits*. He also made wooden rocking toys of dogs and other animals, which sold in major London stores.

He produced advertising material for famous brands such as Colman's Blue and Colman's Starch, Cadbury's Cocoa and, of course, Teacher's Highland Cream. The pictures shown here and on the previous pages show the original artwork from the 1920s for public-house advertisement boards of a Man Playing Golf, Men Curling and Hunting themes.

In the Teacher's archives is a copy of a small book containing Robert Burns' poem "Tam O'Shanter", illustrated by John Faed RSA and some of the original illustrations. This appears to have been published as a promotional tool in the very early 1900s as it bears the inscription "With Wm Teacher & Sons' Compliments", that is before Teacher's became a limited company in 1921. An article entitled "Reminiscences of the late John Faed, RSA" by John Wilson appeared in the *Kikcudbrightshire Advertiser*, dated 12 February 1926. John Wilson described John Faed as,

> *"one of the talented family of painters whose names are deeply engraved in the annals of Galloway … From their earliest youth the Faeds showed the unerring power of portraying nature in all its ever-changing moods, finding amid the unrivalled haunts of childhood the very birthplace of beauty unstained and unadorned."*

The tale of Tam O'Shanter illustrated by John Faed RSA for Wm Teacher & Sons.

A well-known graphic artist in the 1920s and 1930s, Tom Gilfillan produced posters for Teacher's, LMS Railways and McBrayne's steamers among others.

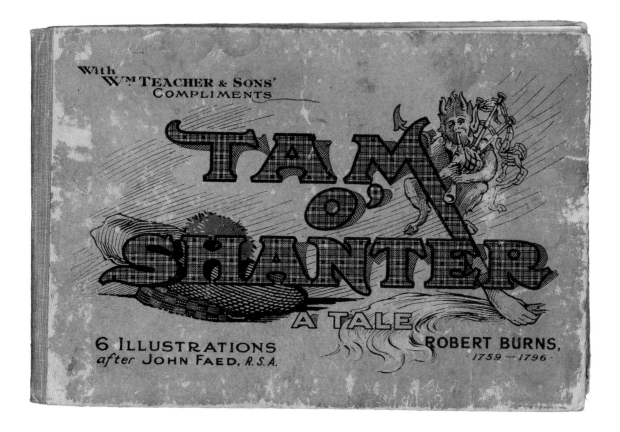

John Faed talked about the gift of being able to paint, *"How often have I felt like the alchemist who has found by research some new and wonderful discovery when a rarer flower or stone than usual rewarded my long hunt fully many miles afield."* John Faed lived at Ardmore near Gatehouse of Fleet – a remarkable coincidence given the name of Teacher's key distillery. As will be seen throughout the following chapters, buying and commissioning art would continue to be an abiding interest for the company.

The third thread is charitable donations. We have heard how William Teacher looked after Robert Barr and supported the Chartist and Temperance Movements and Cancer Research, and that Adam Teacher donated a considerable sum to Glasgow charities. Donations to charity continue to play an important part in the community life of Teacher's Highland Cream where employees select their charity and raise their own funds, then matched by the company.

ESTD · WM TEACHER & SONS · GLASGOW · 1830

THE RIGHT SPIRITS BOYS AND PROHIBITION

From an archivist's point of view, looking at items from the period 1920–60 is like uncovering a rich seam of wonderful advertisements. For the first time it appears that Wm Teacher & Sons decided to keep a record of their publicity and promotional activities. The reason for this could be that up until then the need to advertise had not been so important. By 1920 there were other brand leaders in the marketplace and companies such as DCL were flexing their muscles.

Some of the advertisements may have been kept for curiosity, such as those of 1922 suggesting that you can combat influenza: "Good Scotch Whisky is the best preventative beforehand, and good Red Wine is the best restorative afterwards".

Both, of course, were available from William Teacher's! (These advertisements would have been created in response to the 1918 Spanish flu epidemic, which killed 22 million people around the world.) Teacher's did, however, stop far short of the claims made in *Hollinshed's Chronicles* of 1577 on the Virtues of Whisky. Hollinshed reckoned that whisky would help all sorts of things if taken moderately. The long list included stopping *"the guts from rumblying, the hands from shivering and the stomach from womblyng"*, not to mention helping digestion.

The story of the "Right Spirit Boys" has been told many times before, but no book on the history of Teacher's advertising would be complete without retelling it. In 1926 a photographer working for the *Sunday Pictorial* magazine took a picture of two little boys playing cricket in a London street with a wicket made of three empty bottles. One of the wickets was an empty Teacher's whisky bottle. The directors of Teacher's saw the

INFLUENZA

Good Scotch Whisky is the best preventative beforehand, and good Red Wine the best restorative afterwards.

"HIGHLAND CREAM,"

Perfection of old Scotch Whisky,

Per **12/6** Bottle.

"FINEST SPANISH,"

Per **2/-** Bottle.

Highest Quality Tarragona Red Wine.

...lishments.

& SONS.

Glasgow Herald 9/3/22

"HIGHLAND CREAM."

PERFECTION OF OLD SCOTCH WHISKY.

12/6 PER BOTTLE; 150/- PER DOZEN.

FINEST SPANISH RED WINE.

2/- PER BOTTLE; 24/- PER DOZEN.

OBTAINABLE FROM OUR RETAIL ESTABLISHMENTS.

450 ARGYLE STREET.
144 ST GEORGE'S ROAD.
134 NEW CITY ROAD.
282 CROWN STREET.

IN WHOLESALE QUANTITIES (NOT LESS THAN 2 GALLONS OR 12 BOTTLES).

AT 14 ST ENOCH SQUARE.

WM. TEACHER & SONS.

NZA

...tive beforehand, and ...ve afterwards.

...REAM,"

...isky.

"FINEST SPANISH,"

Per **2/-** Bottle.

Highest Quality Tarragona Red Wine.

...Establishments.

& SONS.

INFLUENZA

Good Scotch Whisky is the best preventative beforehand, and good Red Wine the best restorative afterwards.

"HIGHLAND CREAM,"

Perfection of old Scotch Whisky.

Per **12/6** Bottle.

"FINEST SPANISH,"

Per **2/-** Bottle.

Highest Quality Tarragona Red Wine.

OBTAINABLE AT ALL OUR RETAIL ESTABLISHMENTS.

WM. TEACHER & SONS.

photograph and thought it would make a good advertisement for their brand. Teacher's decided to find the two boys and discovered they were Charlie and Frank Smith. At the time of the photograph Charlie was six and his younger brother four. Teacher's contacted the boys' mother in Brixton, London and agreed to pay her an annual allowance of £5 to help her bring up the two boys. So began a long association with the boys' family and a highly successful advertising campaign.

The company retains all the correspondence between Mrs Smith and the Directors. In one of the annual letters dated 22 June 1939 the company wrote, 'We take pleasure again in sending you £10 which we hope will enable you to take a holiday with your family." In those days £10 would have been more than enough for a holiday, when the price of a bottle of Teacher's Highland Cream retailed at around three shillings and sixpence. Teacher's kept in touch with Mrs Smith, including sending her flowers when she was unwell, until she died in December 1978, aged 92. This has echoes of the story, already told in Chapter 1, of the tailor Robert Barr and his Teacher's pension.

Teacher's celebrated its centenary with a series of pictures in 1930. The "Right Spirit Boys" were featured on a poster and a green metal tray to commemorate the centenary and they continued to appear on advertisements and promotional material right up until the 1950s. The centenary poster shows the two boys handing their teacher, complete with mortarboard and gown, a wooden case containing Teacher's whisky. Certainly a different take on

Reprint of Trade Press Advertisement.

an apple for the teacher! Today, it is impossible to use children in this way to publicise alcoholic drink. The boys appeared on other items produced during this period, including a Christmas box set with the "Right Spirit Boys" on the inside of the lid of the three-bottle wooden gift carton. Teacher's also launched the first of a series of water jugs in the 1930s, some with the boys on the side, others with the Teacher head logo. The production of water jugs for promotional purposes continues to this day.

Some of the promotional material also harks back to a different time. Teacher's produced a series of blotting-paper sheets including centenary examples showing the "Right Spirit Boys" with their teacher. Others showed Sir Walter Scott, Tam O'Shanter and Gladstone – a real political and literary mix here. And a third series concentrated on the distilling process. Today, the need for paper to blot letters handwritten in ink has largely been superseded by the biro and laptop computer.

Photo-history of Teacher's Water Jugs with examples from 1930 to 1996.

Blotting paper sheets celebrating 10,000 cases of Teacher's whisky travelling to London by train, the introduction of the new 'Self-Opening Bottle' and the 'Right Spirit Boys'.

TEACHER'S HIGHLAND CREAM

Every Drop a bit of Scotland

With Compliments
WM. TEACHER & SONS, LTD.,
DISTILLERS,
GLASGOW & LONDON

SELF-OPENING BOTTLE

CONTENTS GUARANTEED
⅛ OF A GALLON OR 5⅓ GILLS

TEACHER'S   IS   THE LARGEST *INDEPENDENT* WHISKY BUSINESS

WM. TEACHER & SONS, LTD, DISTILLERS GLASGOW & LONDON
ESTAB. 1830.

"Know, foolish Saracen," replied the Christian without hesitation, "that thou blasphemest the gifts of God, even with the blasphemy of thy father Ishmael. The juice of the grape is given to him that will use it wisely, as that which cheers the heart of man after toil, refreshes him in sickness and comforts him in sorrow. He who so enjoyeth it may thank God for his wine-cup as for his daily bread; and he who abuseth the gift of Heaven is not a greater fool in his intoxication than thou in thine abstinence."

—SCOTT

Sir Walter Scott

TEACHER'S is the largest INDEPENDENT Scotch Whisky Business

WM. TEACHER & SONS, LTD.,   DISTILLERS,   GLASGOW & LONDON

"TEACHER" BOTTLING PLANT
(EXPORT DEPARTMENT)
THE "WYLIE" NAILING MACHINES

AFTER each case is filled, it is passed to one of our Nailing Machines as illustrated hereon, and the nailing of the lid is completed in two strokes.

These Machines automatically feed and drive up to six nails at each stroke.

All our Nailing Machines are fitted with special Auxiliary Ball-Bearing Tables which render the handling of the filled cases easy, and reduce the risk of breakage.

Each Machine is capable of nailing 250 cases an hour, or, say—4 per minute. They are mounted on special Roller-Bearing Wheels, and, being fitted with self-contained Electric Motor Drive, can be moved and operated in any desired position.

SELF-OPENING BOTTLE

CONTENTS GUARANTEED
⅛ OF A GALLON OR 5⅓ GILLS

TEACHER'S   IS   THE LARGEST *INDEPENDENT* WHISKY BUSINESS

Blotting paper sheets also featured famous Scots and the art of distillation.

£75,000 of Teacher's Highland Cream on its way to London from Glasgow 11 March 1929.

The Temperance Movement in the UK may have made a difference to the sales of alcohol. Full-scale Prohibition, which came into force in January 1920 in the USA, had a more devastating effect on sales. The First World War had an impact on the production of alcohol, for the most part because cereals were needed to produce food. In France absinthe was banned in 1915, although this was probably more as a result of pressure from the wine industry, and the Russians stopped selling vodka. Canada prohibited the sale of drinks with an alcoholic content of over 2.5 degrees proof after the War in 1918. This was repealed again on 1 January 1920 to coincide with the introduction of Prohibition across the border.

The Prohibition movement in the United States was fuelled by the Women's Christian Temperance Union's activities during the War. The main protagonist was Wayne Wheeler who was behind the Anti-Saloon League, but the 18th Amendment, which was put to Congress, was presented by a Republican congressman from Minnesota, Andrew J. Volstead. The Volstead Act prohibited the "Manufacture, sale and transportation of intoxicating liqueurs banned by constitutional amendment in the US".

At the start of Prohibition, gangsters and bootleggers took over from legitimate businesses and all kinds of dubious spirits were being sold under the counter and behind closed doors.

Prohibition lasted longer than many predicted and by 1923 even businesses, such as Wm Teacher & Sons, who prided themselves on dealing legitimately, started to look at ways of exporting whisky to the United States.

Prohibition was to make several changes to the way people drank. The cocktail, which had been around since the 16th century, gained a new lease of life, principally because of the necessity to hide the rawness of some of the alcohol available. Strangely those who could afford to buy, or indeed were lucky enough to have access to the real thing, also drank cocktails. Bartenders started experimenting with different flavours and when they were able once again to use good whisky, such as Teacher's, produced new exciting cocktails.

The new breed of bar or speakeasy was open to both male and female drinkers. Previously Prohibition bars had been for men only. The bars were also designed to create a very different atmosphere:

> *"Dark and guarded doors opening into a spreading world of enchantment; a world of soft lights, seductive scents, silken music, adroit entertainment, smoke and laughter, of perfection of food and service, of wines and liquors of the first quality, all in a setting of gold and silver and brocade, velvet, iron, glass and exotic woods."*

The consumption of Irish whisky declined during Prohibition. Before Prohibition, locally made whisky and Irish were most freely available. Bootleggers passed off their own backyard distillates as Irish, and this led to a backlash from which the Irish distillers would never properly recover. Scotch whisky trade increased during Prohibition and even companies like Teacher's, with their reputation for honesty and fair play, found ways of getting their stocks through to their customers.

William Manera Bergius, then Export Director, writes,

> *"The American bootleg trade started about 1921, but at first was very chancy, and in the hands of disreputable people, so we paid no heed to it. However, we made our first shipment (to Vancouver) in 1923, refusing to tie ourselves up with anyone, and insisting upon cash before shipment. We did an increasing trade as the years passed, our biggest single shipment being 18,000 cases (in 1929). All this whisky was sack packed, and our success was largely due to the efficiency of our sack packing, which reduced breakage to a minimum. To realise how serious losses by breakage were, one has only to reflect that every bottle found broken on arrival at, for instance, New York, meant a loss of £2 or £3!*

> *"I said, 'We are doing good work in this illegal business. We are letting the Americans have good Scotch whisky to drink in place of their own somewhat poisonous distillations, and we are bringing good American money into this impoverished old country.'"*

Teacher's also used the services of Joseph Hobbs who made his fortune transporting whisky from Canada into the United States. He used his own boat, *Littlehorn*, to bring a total of 137,927 cases of Teacher's Highland Cream down the coast to San Francisco.

But it was not all good news. In 1922 the UK government increased the rate of duty to £3 12s. 6d. a gallon, which prohibited the expansion of the Home Trade market. William Manera reported that consumption, *"... decreased considerably. We have, however, held our place and that without the expensive advertising of our competitors."* Also in 1929, before the end of Prohibition in 1933, the American economy sank into depression and the Wall Street Crash was followed by a period of high taxation and low employment. This was to affect the economies of the rest of the world and with increasing pressure on its resources, the UK economy also collapsed.

As Prohibition started to unravel, all Scotch Whisky manufacturers looked for new agents. Teacher's appointed Messrs Schieffelin & Co of New York in 1931. In 1933 Teacher's celebrated shipping their first consignment post Prohibition on the Cunard Steamer *Scythia*.

America wasn't the only export market. An article in *The Wine & Spirit Trade Record* of 14 June 1932 reported of the success of the Scottish Trade Mission Ship *Leititia*'s visit to Canada. It "was a floating exhibition of the manufactures Scotland can offer not only to the Dominions, but to the whole world." The article includes a photograph of the Messrs Wm Teacher and Sons, Ltd stand which included a model of Ardmore distillery and copies of the company's leaflet *The Virtues of Whisky*.

The first post-Prohibition shipment destined for the USA leaving King Street, December 1933.

SCHIEFFELIN IN AMERICA, THE SECOND WORLD WAR AND LADIES

Schieffelin, Teacher's US agent, kept a record of advertisements from the magazines in which they appeared. And, what's more, they kept the editorial copy alongside, so we have some wonderful glimpses into history. The American advertisements had two consistent themes. The first was "The Right Spirit" and the second "It's the Flavour".

1935 advertisement for the American market.

"It's the flavour"

Teacher's is a man's Scotch, with an honest, hearty taste.

Its tang has a mellow mildness that instantly appeals. For friendly times . . . and any times . . . it

is the connoisseur's choice. The men who demand good whisky are the best friends Teacher's has.

Made since 1830 by Wm. Teacher & Sons, Ltd., Glasgow and London.   *Sole Agents for the United States:* Schieffelin & Co., New York City.   Importers since 1794

In all cases the Teacher's head logo appeared in a small roundel at the bottom of the page next to the bottle and often the words "86 Proof".

A typical advertisement from 1935 reads as follows:

> *"Forget the century-old background of Teacher's Highland Cream Scotch Whisky … forget that it is made by the largest independent distilling house in all Great Britain … forget that it is a worldwide favorite … judge it solely on its merits, its satin smoothness, its mellowness, its full body and rich flavour … Distilled, aged and bottled in Scotland by Wm Teacher & Sons Ltd, Glasgow and London – 'The Right Spirit'."*

Another campaign was created around the theme of Glasgow teashops, of which there were many at the time. One advertisement shows an elderly gentleman being asked if he would like "Tea, Sir?" by a pretty young lady and replying, "Tea? Me? No! Teacher's", the copy comes from *Colliers* magazine of 14 December 1936. This advertisement was also used for the Home Market.

The 1936 advertisements for the American market followed very much the Scottish Highland theme with kilted gentlemen and phrases such as "The most important factor in the worldwide popularity of Teacher's Highland Cream Scotch Whisky is its flavour, reminiscent of fragrant peat fires and mountain heather …" Or how about, "There's no music so blithesome as that of a bagpipe … and whisky with a flavour to match that of Teacher's Highland Cream"?

From time to time humour is used, such as a picture of two old gentlemen in *Time* magazine on 23 March 1936, one of whom is paying for the whisky, clearly an infrequent event as the caption reads, "I see ye're na' sae r-relooctant, Jamie, when it's Teacher's".

There is absolutely no doubt about the target audience for this advertising. The copy for an advertisement in 1938 runs, "Teacher's is a man's Scotch … The men who demand good whisky are the best friends Teacher's has." Others state that "Men appreciate Teacher's for Christmas … Give a man this Scotch he will like …" There is no suggestion that women might enjoy a glass of whisky.

During the same period, in spite of the Home Trade problems, there was some advertising. The recurring themes of "Perfection of Old Scotch" and "It's the Flavour" appear. One, in 1932, refers to the fact that "Teacher's Bottles are – securely stoppered, easy to open, convenient to close again …" Teacher's "Family Price Lists" featured on a regular basis in the *Glasgow Press*.

After Prohibition and the American Depression things started to get back to normal. By 1938 Teacher's was the number one blended whisky brand in the USA market. But then the Second World War started and the Ministry of Food cut malt whisky distilling by

one-third in 1940 and supplies of whisky for consumption in the home trade were reduced by 20 per cent, freeing up whisky for overseas trade.

The same year, 1940, was a boom year for exports, particularly to America, but again outside influences were to stop the lucrative trade. Constant attacks on British shipping by the enemy reduced the number of voyages across the Atlantic. Some vessels did manage

Teacher's Family
Price List
28 December 1929
shows the company's
ten branches.

TEACHER

WM. TEACHER & SONS, LTD. respectfully request their customers, where possible, to make their purchases on MONDAY, as on Tuesday, the 31st (Hogmanay), the pressure of business becomes very great, and causes much disappointment to customers who may thereby be prevented from making their purchases.

ALL LICENSED PREMISES WILL REMAIN CLOSED ON WEDNESDA. (NEW YEAR'S DAY).

FAMILY PRICE LIST

SPIRITS

	Bottle	Half-Bott.	Gill
HIGHLAND CREAM	12/6	6/3	2/8
(Perfection of Old Scotch Whisky)			
FINE OLD IRISH, 43% under proof	10/-	5/-	2/-
RUM, Finest Old	10/-	5/-	2/-
GIN, Hollands, Loopuyt's	12/6	—	2/6
BRANDY, Hennessy 1900	16/3	8/2	3/3
(Labelled "Liqueur Brandy")			

3d. returned on bottles.   1d. on half-bottles.

WINES

	Bottle	Half-Bott.	Gill
SPECIAL SPANISH, N.E., 42%	3/-	1/7	7d
(Specially shipped for us.)			

1d. returned on bottles.

	Quarter-Gall.	Bottle	Half-Bott.	Gill
TEACHER'S BRITISH WINE, N.E., 29%	2/6	1/8	10d.	4d.
Bottles charged	3d.	1d.	1d.	—
(Made specially for us, and sold only in our own shops.)				

		Bottle	Half-Bott.	Gill
PORT, No. 8	N.E., 42%	5/-	2/7	1/-
PORT, No. 5	N.E., 42%	3/10	2/-	9d.
SHERRY, Fine Old	N.E., 42%	3/10	2/-	9d.
CLARET, Fine Bordeaux		2/-	1/1	—

1d. returned on bottles.

Wm. TEACHER & SONS Ltd.

ESTABLISHED 1830

SOLE PROPRIETORS, ARDMORE DISTILLERY, KENNETHMONT

Importers of Wines and Foreign Spirits

BRANCHES

45 YORK STREET	Corner STIRLING ROAD
450 ARGYLE STREET	and BARONY STREET
57 CLYDE STREET	Corner RUTHERGLEN ROAD
607 ARGYLE STREET	and S. WELLINGTON ST.
(Foot of North Street)	Corner CUMBERLAND STREET
144 ST. GEORGE'S ROAD	and CROWN STREET
134 NEW CITY ROAD	Corner CUMBERLAND STREET
	and SALISBURY STREET

to get across, principally funded by the National Association of Beverage Importers. Many of the advertisements mentioned above continued to appear during the war and Schieffelin & Co. imported Teacher's whisky, albeit in limited quantities.

"Here's tae th' kilt, An 'th' loch an' th' heather, Here's tae th'friends, Ne'er known as 'fair-weather" is the toast made in an advertisement in 1941 next to a really exciting article "Out of the Night" about sabotage of Japanese ships in dockyards in Europe. This is reproduced in full so that the reader can follow that stage of the story – I would love to know what happened to Mr Chang.

One of the advertisements with the headline "Tae anither-r Yuletide!" appears in a 1942 copy of a magazine, believed to be *The New Yorker*, alongside an article about rationing and price control. For the hard-pressed British public who saw American GIs as fairy godfathers with sweets and silk stockings in their pockets, it might have been heart-warming to know that things weren't all that easy across the Atlantic as well.

The advertisement "Nae mair need be said!" is opposite an article with a photograph of an oil-covered diver on the deck of the battleship *Arizona* about the 1943 resurrection of wrecked American warships at Pearl Harbour. The article goes on to say that,

> "… *many US battleships, shattered by bomb and torpedo on 7 December 1941 and subsequently refloated and rebuilt, have been sent back to the war as better fighting ships than they were when sunk. Of the 19 ships damaged on that fateful day, 14 have already been repaired and sent to sea under their own power. Three of the remaining five, the* Arizona, Oklahoma *and* Utah, *are at present undergoing salvage operations.* "The remaining two, the destroyers Cassin *and* Downes, *were damaged beyond economical repair but more than 50 per cent of their equipment has been utilized in new ship construction. This record has bettered anything the Navy dared hope when it made a preliminary survey of the smoking ruins a few hours after the attack.*"

The *Arizona* was, in fact, never salvaged and remains a memorial to this day.

Gentlemen at leisure playing billiards, polo and other sports was a popular theme.

Another 1943 example is a larger half-page advertisement with the headline caption "Oop wi'our glasses … th'better tae see our absent friends" and two kilted gentlemen toasting each other. The article this time talks about Revolution in Mass Production. This discusses the vexed question of whether the smaller manufacturer can afford to buy expensive machinery to mechanize his plant or whether he can afford not to, as either way he will be squeezed out of the marketplace altogether. The question of the elimination of manual labour seems to have become more a matter of *when* rather than of *whether* (see following page).

The 1944 advertisement "Auld Scots remember-r-r!" is next to an article about General Bradley with a photograph of Eisenhower, Churchill and Bradley trying out their abilities on the army range. Apparently *"Bradley is easily the best, being able to kill a pheasant with a .22 caliber rifle."*

At the end of the Second World War things slowly got back to normal. However, whisky production had been severely reduced as most whisky distilleries were forced to close from 1941 onwards. Imports of grain ceased and any grain produced in the UK was destined to feed the hungry population as rationing increased. Some people speculated on existing whisky stocks, which were sold at high prices. In 1944, when the government felt that the tide was turning, and that the UK might win the war the restrictions were

Revolution in Mass Production
[*Continued from page 205*]

insist that the small fellow—if mechanized—can match the efficiency of the big plant and at the same time meet its competition. But mechanization is expensive, and the need to purchase machines is urgent. It is not a question of buying a materials-handling machine now, a second machine later, an additional machine still later. It is often a question of buying an entire system of machines now or never. There is little room for, say, an auto manufacturer who can't finance an assembly line. One engineer states flatly that he has never made a materials-handling installation that has not paid for itself in three years. Yet these earlier installations benefit from the high unit cost of industries not generally converted to mechanical carriers. Methods of financing smaller purchases must be created if smaller factories are not to be crowded out. It should be emphasized that materials-handling systems are available for small as well as large plants.

Materials-handling systems may work miracles in volume production, but they work better when products are rigidly standardized. A well-integrated factory in which production machines and material-flow machines are carefully meshed must close down, redesign, and retool its entire plant—not a single department of it—every time there is a change in the blueprints; automobile plants, for example, must close every year to change their products. For plants that have been making industrial products to specifications the machine handling of materials will bring great changes, inasmuch as such plants can hardly retool for every new order. Standardization, with all the business changes attendant upon it, will probably not be impressed upon manufacturers of variety products, however, since the more rigid systems of production flow require heavy volume production.

The question of the elimination of manual labor seems to have become more a matter of *when* than of *whether*. Production machinery has already robbed labor of many of its skilled functions. Handling machinery, by its ability to carry a piece of work from one workman to the next, makes possible the breaking up of complex jobs into a series of minor operations. What is more, it reduces in number and simplifies the work of men who formerly carried the materials to the machines and to the trucks, railroads, and steamships. Skilled labor goes, manual labor goes; the world's goods are produced by the semiskilled. There will be fewer men needed just when the size of the potential labor supply is greatest—for the factory is now as much a place for women as for men. The early steam shovels, which required a crew of ten, did almost ten times as much work as ten men with hand shovels; today's machine shovels, which have only a couple of attendants, can handle ten times as much as the earlier ones.

There will be more capacity to produce, but there will be fewer jobs to fill. Materials handling is not going to produce depressions; but it can very possibly make depressions more severe. It dramatizes the urgency for finding basic solutions for our economic problems, and for matching mass production of goods with mass *distribution* of goods.

Probably no single thing emphasizes so pointedly the human problem, perhaps the spiritual problem, of man's labor as the difference between the old lathe and the new assembly line. The assembly line is not a place for the stupid; it wants bright but semiskilled persons; refuses simple jobs to the simpler minds; and demands the best human material for the most repetitive machine work. The engineer, the tool and product designer, becomes the last craftsman. Men's reasoning and creativity become the playthings of idle hours. The machines will fetch, carry, and produce. Man must work his own salvation.

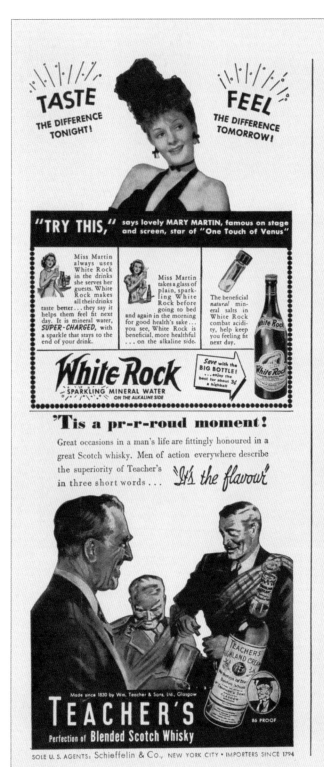
"Yank" (continued)

IT IS AT ITS BEST IN CARTOONS

The outstanding quality of the American doughboy, wherever he may be fighting, is his raucous sense of humor. It is reflected in the funny stories, cartoons and the burly jokes of his Army papers. As might be expected, the humorous sections of these papers are the best sections. *Yank* is at its best when printing cartoons like the ones which are reproduced below.

"THEY SAY THEY DON'T NEED ANY PARACHUTES—THEY'RE MARINES"

"WADDA YUH MEAN, YOU'D LIKE TO SEE THE HEAD WAITER!"

RECRUIT   AFTER BASIC TRAINING   CORPORAL   SERGEANT

IN ART.
EXPERIENCE IS THE GREAT TEACHER

IN SCOTCH...
TEACHER'S
IS THE GREAT EXPERIENCE

Milton Caniff, creator of "Steve Canyon."

Only experience could produce Scotch of such unvarying
quality and good taste as Teacher's Highland Cream.
Today, the fourth and fifth generations of the Teacher
family still personally supervise the making of this
famous product of Wm. Teacher & Sons, Ltd.

TEACHER'S HIGHLAND CREAM BLENDED SCOTCH WHISKY / 86 PROOF
SCHIEFFELIN® & CO., NEW YORK, N.Y.

IN SAILING...
EXPERIENCE IS THE GREAT TEACHER

IN SCOTCH...
TEACHER'S
IS THE GREAT EXPERIENCE

Colin E. Ratsey, world famous sailmaker, Vice President of Ratsey & Lapthorn Sailmakers, Inc.

All the experience and resources of the firm
Wm. Teacher & Sons, Ltd. are concentrated on producing
<u>one quality</u> of Scotch whisky — Teacher's Highland
Cream. The Teacher family has personally supervised
the making of this famous brand since 1830.

TEACHER'S HIGHLAND CREAM BLENDED SCOTCH WHISKY / 86 PROOF
SCHIEFFELIN® & CO., NEW YORK, N.Y.

lifted and some grain was released for distilling. Winston Churchill believed strongly that whisky distilling should start as soon as possible for export purposes. In April 1945 he said that *"On no account reduce the barley for whisky. This takes years to mature and is an invaluable export and dollar producer. Having regard to all our other difficulties about export, it would be most improvident not to preserve this characteristic British element of ascendancy."* (This quotation comes from one of Churchill's memos and appears in, among others, *Scotch: Its History and Romance.*)

It wasn't to be a peaceful world after the Second World War. Britain continued to be involved in Malaysia and Burma and the Americans in Korea. The Korean War (1950–53) was between North Korea, aided by Communist China and South Korea and helped by the US and other members of the United Nations. From 1959 Vietnam was to be dominated by war between the Communist Viet Cong, supported by North Vietnam, and the South Vietnamese Government with increasing assistance from US troops. Demonstrations against the war were to continue throughout the 1960s, which dragged on until a peace agreement was reached in 1973.

The start of another innovative advertising campaign in the United States began in 1959. This featured personalities in various walks of life, a theme that would be repeated later. The theme was Experience. So for Colin E. Ratsey, world-famous sailmaker, the headline was "In Sailing … Experience is the Great Teacher, In Scotch … Teacher's is the Great Experience." This was repeated for Milton Caniff, the creator of the Steve Canyon cartoon figure as "In Art … Experience is the Great Teacher", and for Alan Livingston, Vice President in charge of Creative Services at Capitol Records, as "In Recording … Experience is the Great Teacher."

The 1960s "Water" campaign was to herald a change in the previously male-oriented copy. It is, however, perhaps still a little patronising for today's female reader:

"Clever You to Give Him Water with Teacher's Highland Cream Scotch Whisky … that makes it a 'must' on your weekly shopping list! Fifty-fifty … water and Teacher's! … You and the man in your life will agree that water and unforgettable Teacher's is *the* drink for memorable moments." Or how about, "Why do men love women who love men who love … Teacher's Highland Cream Scotch Whisky?"

From the UK in the 1960s there's an advertisement of a gentleman with a cigarette and a glass of whisky discussing the merits of whisky. This is reproduced here and for easy reading the copy is also given below:

"Ladies … You'll see below just why men like Teacher's so. And you'll quickly learn to like Teacher's, too. Your publican, licensed grocer or off-licence is your friend and an expert on whisky. Ask him about Teacher's Highland Cream. Make a shopping note now to buy a gay red half-bottle pack of unforgettable Teacher's. Just 19s. 6d. with the

IN BOWLING...

EXPERIENCE IS THE GREAT TEACHER

IN SCOTCH...

TEACHER'S

IS THE GREAT EXPERIENCE

Andy Varipapa, bowling champion and member of Bowling Hall of Fame.

In Teacher's Highland Cream you have the end result of 130 years of experience in doing just one thing to perfection: creating a Scotch with unmistakable flavour and character. Making Teacher's has been a family craft since 1830 and its distinctive formula is strictly adhered to by William Teacher's three great-great grandsons.

It's the flavour...unmistakable

TEACHER'S
HIGHLAND CREAM SCOTCH WHISKY

BOTTLED IN SCOTLAND

BLENDED SCOTCH WHISKY/86 PROOF/SCHIEFFELIN & CO., NEW YORK

IN MUSIC...
EXPERIENCE IS THE GREAT TEACHER

IN SCOTCH...
TEACHER'S
IS THE GREAT EXPERIENCE

Arthur Fiedler, famous conductor and exclusive RCA recording artist.

Only experience could produce such a superb Scotch as
Teacher's Highland Cream. Wm. Teacher & Sons, Ltd.
has made this fine Scotch since 1830. The firm
is still personally controlled and managed by the
fourth and fifth generations of the Teacher family.

BOTTLED IN
SCOTLAND

TEACHER'S HIGHLAND CREAM BLENDED SCOTCH WHISKY / 86 PROOF
SCHIEFFELIN® & CO., NEW YORK, N.Y.

unique screw-top 12-tot measuring cap that makes Teacher's so easy to serve. Fifty-fifty with … water and Teacher's. Simply superb and superbly simple! This weekend, share Teacher's secret with the man in your life!"

"I just can't understand other men's wives … and that's the way my wife says to keep it! But it does annoy me when we're invited out … to have the hostess serve me an insipid drink. My wife knows that Teacher's is the drink men really want! Every time I inhale

It's
a
sobering
and
somewhat
melancholy
thought . . .
that
the
time
you're
now
taking
to
read
about
it
could
be
spent
enjoying
the
unmistakable
flavour
and
warmth
of
Teacher's
Highland
Cream.

There's
more
to
be
said
for
one
bottle
of
Teacher's
than
a
case
of
ordinary
whisky

TEACHER'S HIGHLAND CREAM
is now back in full supply. Enjoy
this cream of Scotch Whisky today!

TEACHER'S HIGHLAND CREAM
is now back in full supply. Enjoy
this cream of Scotch Whisky today!

Christmas

is a

time to

give

and

take . . .

a time to

give

and

take

unmistakable

Teacher's

Highland

Cream!

Isn't it

wonderful

that

364 days

a year—

and

Christmas

too—

you and

your friends

can enjoy

unmistakable

Teacher's!

TEACHER'S HIGHLAND CREAM
is now back in full supply. Available
in the gay new half-bottle pack at just
19/6—or in standard bottle. Enjoy this
Cream of Scotch Whisky today!

TEACHER'S HIGHLAND CREAM
so well worth looking for. Available
in the gay new half-bottle pack at just
19/6—or in standard bottle. Enjoy this
Cream of Scotch Whisky today!

Once
upon a time
a wee
Teacher's
had to
go
a long
way
but that's
all
over
now

TEACHER'S HIGHLAND CREAM
We can now supply your orders.
Wm. Teacher & Sons Ltd.
St. Enoch Square, Glasgow C.1.

It wasn't easy to say "NO" for 24 years...

IN 1937, Teacher's Highland Cream was the leading Scotch whisky in America...a leadership attributable to Teacher's traditional policy that Quality must always prevail over Quantity ...that only exceptionally fine Scotch could ever bear the Teacher's name.

DESPITE a vigorous expansion program planned to satisfy the growing world market, the tremendous demand for Teacher's outstripped the firm's ability to supply their quality whisky.

TO the suggestion that Teacher's Highland Cream meet the demand by varying its quality...the Board of Directors gave an unequivocal "no"...a "no" that has endured 24 years and has kept Teacher's in limited supply throughout the world.

But now ...

MR. RONALD M. TEACHER, Chairman of the Board, reveals he is confident that the firm has now sufficient stocks so that Teacher's can once again be in free supply in the United States.

SO now at last your retailer can supply you with Teacher's by the case or fill an order for as many bottles as you wish. Perhaps you were very young 25 years ago, if so, why not try something that has been worth waiting for.

It's the flavour...unmistakable

TEACHER'S
HIGHLAND CREAM SCOTCH WHISKY

| BOTTLED IN SCOTLAND |

BLENDED SCOTCH WHISKY / 86 PROOF / SCHIEFFELIN & CO., NEW YORK

its tantalizing bouquet … Every time I tempt my palate with a sip … Every time I enjoy the sheer exhilaration of Teacher's … I know … and she knows … we've made the perfect choice."

This advertisement is the start of a comprehensive campaign about taking Teacher's with water. There are least 40 different advertisements, mostly black and white, featuring a bowler-hatted gentleman with an umbrella. Some are lineage only as the examples on page 115 show. Some of them are quite humorous, for example one shows the bowler-hatted gentleman sitting on a camel by Nelson's Column and the fountains in Trafalgar Square which exhorts the readers to celebrate New Year (1962) "This year stick to water fifty-fifty with Teacher's Highland Cream – the cream of Scotch Whisky … tonight and for the next 364 days."

In 1961 there was a spoof on a pretentious whisky or wine-taster, entitled "the fine art of Water Tasting" – clearly things have not changed that much since then! Another says that "It's a vintage year for Water so enjoy it … fifty-fifty with Teacher's Highland Cream Scotch Whisky."

Teacher's Whisky stocks returned to their pre-war levels in 1962 after years of restrictions and reduced production. One of the home-market advertisements shows a giraffe's neck with the headline "Once upon a time a wee Teacher's had to go a long way but that's all over now", and the comment "We can now supply your orders". The American advertisement had much more copy with the headline, "It wasn't easy to say NO for 24 years".

TEACHER'S GO PUBLIC AND AN INCREASED SHAREHOLDING

During this period various changes occurred within the Teacher and Bergius families. In 1921 the private limited company Wm Teacher & Sons Ltd was formed with William Manera Bergius and William Curtis Teacher as directors. This followed an offer from DCL to buy the firm's stocks. However, this would have meant the end of Wm Teacher's as a separate company and the partners decided not to sell.

William Manera Bergius recorded this event in *Reminiscences*:

"And so we went along the years till about 1921, when we got hints that the DCL would like to have a talk with us. I visited Mr William H. Ross in Edinburgh, and found that they only wanted our stock and that the price would be about 14 s. The business would come to an end. Well, I got back straight to 'Kilarden' and found that my Senior Partner had imagined in my absence exactly what had taken place, and our joint conclusion was 'what about the employees?' so that was that!"

In 1927 Teacher's issued a series of advertisements in the *Licensed Trade Press* entitled "Combine or Non-Combine". As in the past the company was putting its head above the parapet and encouraging publicans to continue supporting "the leading FREE or independent brand on the market".

William Curtis Teacher and his wife Elizabeth Rowena McNairn had four children. The eldest, William George, initially worked in the business, but as already mentioned was killed in action in 1915. His eldest daughter Maude married Robert Dunlop and both their sons, George and Robert were to join Teacher's. Their second daughter Nora married Alastair Anderson and their son, Ronnie M. Anderson, was also to join the family firm.

William Curtis Teacher's second son, Ronald M. Teacher, joined Teacher's in 1922 after serving an apprenticeship in the offices of a shipping firm Henderson & Co of Glasgow. Ronald Teacher had initially wanted to join the Royal Navy, but the loss of his elder brother, William George, during the First World War changed all that. When he began working at Teacher's he started like everyone in the family, at the bottom as a general clerk. The business at the time was firmly in the hands of William Manera Bergius, William Curtis Teacher and Duncan McPherson who had been with William Teacher & Sons since the early days of the partnership. Ronald joined the board in 1925. He shared his love of the sea with other members of the family and he said he couldn't remember a time when he was not "messing about in boats". He acquired his first yacht *Tringa II* at the age of 19 and was to be Commodore of the Royal Clyde Yacht Club for 32 years. William Curtis Teacher died in 1929 at the age of 65, after a lifetime dogged by ill health.

In 1934 Walter Andrew Bergius joined the family firm. *The Bergius Family Tree* relates that,

> *"Born 6 August 1914, [he] was educated at Kelvinside Academy with the assistance of various governesses and tutors owing to a profound deafness. Entered thereafter his uncle's firm the Bergius Co. Ltd in which he gained an engineering proficiency during a period of 3½ years. At the age of 20 and the invitation of his father he entered the old established firm of William Teacher & Sons Ltd. Became a director in 1941 and in 1949 was engaged in floating a Public Holding Company, Teacher (Distillers) Ltd., to further the family interest on account of obstruction by abnormal taxation: was appointed Managing Director during this period. He married Jean Frances Moncrieffe Kinghorn at Innellan, Argyll in April 1946."*

As with the First World War, Teacher's were to lose another key member of the family in the Second World War. (William) Cecil Bergius, born in 1918, joined the company in the late 1930s. He was clearly destined to join the business and was learning as much as he could about it. There are copies of his reports on taking excise samples, the cooper's trade and other aspects of running a whisky company. His input was short-lived, as he died on 1 March 1944 when *HMS Gould*, of which he was Captain, was torpedoed by the enemy.

JULY 15, 1927   THE LICENSED VICTUALLERS' GAZETTE AND HOTEL COURIER.   5

To the Trade

COMBINE OR NON-COMBINE

You will have noticed the intimation in the Press recently of the latest important absorption by the Combine which is threatening to control the Scotch Whisky Trade.

Ours is the leading FREE or independent brand on the market, and we hope that, with the extending support of the trade, we shall continue to afford an alternative source of supply for Scotch Whisky other than the Combine, and thus prevent the creation of an absolute monopoly.

Just as the FREE house claims the support of the consuming public, we think the proprietors of such houses will feel impelled to support the Free Distiller's brand —"TEACHERS."

It is to be hoped sentiment in business is not dead. Our business was established practically a century ago, viz.: in 1830. To-day it is controlled by the grandsons and a great grandson of the Founder, and there are other members of the Family in a younger generation to carry on.

Support TEACHER and TEACHER will support you.

WM. TEACHER & SONS, LTD.

SCOTCH WHISKY DISTILLERS — GLASGOW & LONDON.

On Tuesday 3 August 1943 William Manera Bergius celebrated his business Jubilee with the Company in the board room at 14 St Enoch Square, Glasgow. He was presented with an address printed on vellum with everyone's signatures on it, recording their appreciation for his *"wise guidance, which has steered the business through many difficulties to the successful position it holds today, and your unfailing consideration and kindly treatment of all who have been privileged to serve under you."* The employees also presented him with an oil painting of *Ben Loaghal* by Sir D. Y. Cameron, which had been hung at the Royal Academy.

In 1946 at a celebration of the company's 116th anniversary, William Manera's son, Walter, gave the following speech:

> *"Colonel Young* [Colonel Young was the company lawyer and a partner in the law firm MacRobert Son & Hutchison], *Ladies and Gentlemen. Let me thank Colonel Young for so kindly proposing the toast of Wm Teacher & Sons. The firm is in its 116th year and this happy occasion marks yet another milestone in its long history. It is interesting to look back over these years, and most of you present here can look back a good number of years – I don't mean to suggest years of age, but years of service and connection with the Firm and you will remember that it is not so long ago that we first permitted smoking in the Shops or so long ago that we extended the Bond. These were all milestones also. The firm, along with the rest of the trade, played a big part in the war in that we, by export, brought dollars to this country to finance the War and in supplying the fighting forces with that wee 'Dram' we made life seem rosier when things were very black. It was a big part played by you, all of the firm. Here may I say a word of welcome to those who have returned from the forces and how glad we are to see them back once more. As to the future, restrictions are bound to continue for a number of years yet but after that we can look forward to the good health and prosperity of the Firm."*

The most observant of you will have noted the reference to "permitted smoking in the shops"! So clearly Teacher's had to bow to public demand in the end.

An article appeared on the front page of the *Scottish Daily Express* of 31 December 1948 noting that the directors of William Teacher were putting some of their shares up for sale. Readers will note that there are some inaccuracies in this article. William Teacher Snr did not start a small whisky distillery in Aberdeenshire in 1830, he started a whisky business. The distillery, Ardmore, was not completed until 1898.

> *"Three descendants of William Teacher, who started a small whisky distillery in Aberdeenshire in 1830, will with their friends have a £1,350,000 share out on Thursday, January 13, following sale of a block of shares in the family business – William Teacher & Sons, distillers of 'Highland Cream' Scotch. To William Teacher's great grandsons, Mr Ronald M. Teacher and Mr Walter A. Bergius, and to his grandson Mr William M. Bergius, father of Walter, will go more than £500,000 from the deal. The rest of*

the money, around £85,000, will be shared by several other directors and shareholders who are unnamed in the prospectus offering the shares. The whisky men are selling one million Preference Shares at 21s. 1d. each and 400,000 Ordinary Shares at 15 s. each in their company, letting the public in for the first time … This puts a price label of £2,550,000 on the Teacher business, which until now has had a capital of only £202,000 … The descendants of William Teacher are reluctant sellers. They are cashing their shares only to meet future demands from the taxman, including death duties."

This last line gives the true reason for the sale. As had happened so many times before in the history of Teacher's, the death of a family member made a huge burden on the company's finances.

ESTD · W^M TEACHER & SONS · GLASGOW · 1830

1953 Coronation Year, HM The Queen visits St Enoch Square.

FAREWELL TO THE DRAM SHOPS, THE GLENDRONACH AND "MAKE YOUR OWN SCOTCH WHISKY"

The previous chapter focused on the wealth of advertising launched by the company between 1920 and 1960. During this period a number of key events happened in the UK and to William Teacher's, which affected the growth of the company.

By 1949 Ronald McNairn Teacher had taken over as Chairman of the company. His task was to help Teacher's regain their leading position in the USA and consolidate sales at home and elsewhere.

The year that heralded the end of rationing on all home-grown grain was 1953, and from January 1954 distillers could sell where they wished, although USA was to remain the key market. The aim was to earn as many dollars as possible to repay war loans and inject much-needed revenue into the UK economy. With limited whisky stocks, sales in the home market continued to be rationed until 1959 and sales of deluxe brands were restricted until 1962.

Teacher's celebrated their 125th anniversary by chartering the *TSS Duchess of Hamilton* for a cruise on 19 May 1955. The boat left Broomielaw in Glasgow at 10 a.m., travelling down the Clyde and round the Island of Bute via Tignabruaich and back up to Gourock. Guests returned from Gourock to Glasgow Central Station by train in the evening. During the

cruise, presentations were made to a large number of staff members. Messrs Howell, Boswell and Morgan celebrated 57, 45 and 44 years service with the company respectively and there were 20 others with over 30 years' loyal service. Clearly Wm Teacher & Sons Ltd was a good company to work for and staff turnover was low.

Whilst writing about this period of the company's growth, it is important to remind everyone how closely involved the directors were in the day-to-day running of the business. All mail was opened and read by the directors around a table and then distributed to the relevant departments. This was not uncommon and most businesses worked in this way.

In 1957, to meet the continuing demand for whisky, the Ardmore distillery increased its production capacity. Teacher's were not the only distillers to do this and by 1968 there was simply too much whisky on the marketplace. The increased demand in the export markets had meant that anything a distillery produced could be sold, but by the 1970s this was all over and the industry entered another slump. It had taken some 60 years to recover from the Pattisons' collapse and for families like Teacher's there was an unfortunate sense of déjà vu.

In 1960 Teacher's bought the Glendronach distillery from the Grey Grant family. Glendronach is situated near Huntly in Banffshire and with the distillery came a 1,000-acre farm, complete with Highland cattle. The Glendronach was a natural purchase, as

The
GLENDRONACH
ORIGINAL

YEAR **12** OLD

PURE HIGHLAND MALT
SCOTCH WHISKY

43% vol   e 75 cl

BOTTLED BY THE PROPRIETOR

PRODUCE OF SCOTLAND · THE GLENDRONACH DISTILLERY Cº LIMITED · LICENSED SINCE 1826

FORGUE BY HUNTLY ABERDEENSHIRE SCOTLAND

The
GLENDRONACH
MATURED IN SHERRY CASKS

YEAR **12** OLD

PURE HIGHLAND MALT
SCOTCH WHISKY

40% vol   5 cl

The
GLENDRONACH
ORIGINAL

FIRST LICENSED IN 1826, GLENDRONACH IS ONE OF SCOTLAND'S OLDEST WORKING DISTILLERIES. GREAT CARE HAS BEEN TAKEN TO PURSUE THE USE OF TRADITIONAL METHODS AND MATERIALS, INCLUDING COAL-FIRED STILLS AND WATER FROM LOCAL SPRINGS.

MANY THINGS AFFECT THE FINAL CHARACTER OF A MALT WHISKY. AMONG THESE THE TYPE OF OAK CASK IN WHICH THE WHISKY IS MATURED HAS AN IMPORTANT INFLUENCE. AT GLENDRONACH PLAIN OAK CASKS ARE USED AS WELL AS ONES WHICH HAVE PREVIOUSLY CONTAINED SHERRY.

THE GLENDRONACH ORIGINAL IS MATURED IN A COMBINATION OF PLAIN OAK AND SHERRY CASKS. EACH IMPARTS ITS OWN SUBTLE FLAVOUR TO THE WHISKY, RESULTING IN A CLASSIC, WELL-BALANCED CHARACTER, CLEAN TASTING BUT WITH A FULL, ROUNDED FLAVOUR.

ALSO AVAILABLE IN BOTTLE IS THE GLENDRONACH, MATURED EXCLUSIVELY IN SHERRY CASKS.

5 010093 560003

SOLE PROPRIETOR SINCE 1960 WM. TEACHER & SONS LTD

First licensed in 1826, Glendronach is one of Scotland's oldest working distilleries. Great care has been taken to pursue the use of traditional methods and materials, including coal-fired stills and water from local springs.

Many things affect the final character of a malt whisky. Among these the type of oak cask in which the whisky is matured has an important influence. At Glendronach plain oak casks are used as well as ones which have previously contained sherry.

The Glendronach, Matured in Sherry Casks, is a full-bodied malt whisky, rich in colour, with a well-rounded flavour and a lingering after taste.

Also available in bottle is the Glendronach Original which is matured in a combination of plain oak and sherry casks.

SOLE PROPRIETOR SINCE 1960 WM. TEACHER & SONS LTD.

Wm Teacher & Sons had worked closely with the distillery for a very long time. Readers will recall that James Innes from The Glendronach assisted with the building of Ardmore Distillery. The Glendronach Single Malt Whisky has always been an important part of the Teacher's Highland Cream blend.

Slipping back into the archives we discover press advertisements from the 1950s for the Singapore market. These are a mixture of versions for English-language and Singaporean-language newspapers.

A scrapbook from New Zealand for the 1950s and 1960s shows that Teacher's advertising appeared in eight metropolitan and provincial newspapers in New Zealand each week.

Many of the themes are replicated from other campaigns. At Christmas Teacher's distributed 30,000 copies of a book with advice on being a host entitled *It's an Education* to its provincial agents. The booklet gives us further insight into the brand of Australian Bonded whisky. The introduction peruses the subject of whisky:

> *"Did you know, whisky starts life as beer … and time was, when whisky bottles were corked like wine bottles, to be opened with a corkscrew? Then came Teacher's special stopper, (pre-1967) still on bottles today. Naturally any talk of whisky means mention of William Teacher who set up business in Glasgow, 1830. By 1877, Teacher's were fast expanding. Incidentally during alteration to their offices in Glasgow, staff daily viewed the unusual sight of horses being led through the office from stables at the rear. Now, too, the export trade was well away. A new brand, Australian Bonded whisky, was shipped to Australia to receive the official bonding certificate from that Dominion. On return this Scotch was highly prized, as the sea voyage was held to enhance its natural maturing. Teacher's whisky is even more highly prized today!"*

The book then goes on to describe how to be the perfect host with hints on planning beforehand, having both Teacher's and nibbles to hand and advising that a "tense host relaxes nobody". Finally, there are a few ideas on entertaining your guests, making savouries and how to mix whisky cocktails, such as Highball, Mint Julep, Whisky Collins and Old Fashioned, providing a comprehensive guide to entertaining in style.

In 1954 Teacher's sponsored their first golf tournament, the PGA Seniors Championship in the USA, which was to become a prestigious annual event. Golf was to be an important part of Teacher's Sponsorship activities in both the USA and the UK. Chapter 6 covers other sports sponsorship in the 1980s and 1990s.

Adam Bergius, Walter's younger brother and Export Director of Teacher's Scotch Whisky, got together with Rowland Emett to create a very special book, *Make Your Own Scotch Whisky* in 1960.

The book starts with, "First pipe in a suitable supply of Scottish hill water, and add to this a goodly quantity of barley, allowing it to soak for 48 hours. Then strain off the water, and lay out the wet barley on a cool floor in a great heap. It will start to grow, and in doing so, will become hot. So make a wooden spade, and every few hours turn it over, each time spreading it a little thinner on the floor to keep it cool."

The story continues through the whole cycle of single malt whisky production and continues. "You won't recognise what you have made, but if you are in Scotland, and if you put it in a oak cask and keep it there for three years, then you are legally allowed to call it Scotch Whisky. However, as you have made it outside the law, you will not be allowed to call it anything, and, in fact, you had better keep very quiet about it. If you live elsewhere, you will just have made whisky. It may be good, or it may be bad, for no-one

1960s International
Sales Leaflet by
Roland Emett.

Throughout the world

there's international agreement

on . . .

TEACHER'S

SCOTCH WHISKY

but why?

MAKE YOUR OWN
SCOTCH WHISKY
AT HOME

*A complete
& unabridged
"do-it-yourself"
Guide*

EMETT

Enkele weken geleden had U een ui naar Uw loodgieter moeten sturen en hem moeten vragen deze na te maken in koper, groot genoeg om de "wash" te bevatten. U vult nu de koperen ui en verbindt het uiteinde met een kurketrekkerachtige pijp, die ondergedompeld dient te blijven in stromend water.

Zet een blauwbrander onder de ui en wacht op de druppels, die uit het eind van de pijp komen. Wanneer er niets meer komt, maak dan Uw distilleertoestel leeg en reinig het zorgvuldig. Daarna doet U het eindproduct er weer in en begint opnieuw.

U zult niet weten wat U gemaakt heeft, maar als U in Schotland woont en U doet het in een eiken vat en houdt het daar gedurende drie jaar, dan is het geoorloofd bij de wet om het Schotse whisky

knows what the product of a new distillery will be like until it has been made, matured and tasted, and the different shapes of Stills make different kinds of whisky."

The final paragraph reads, "When Government taxes on whisky are deducted, it is really very inexpensive, and even if you do try to make it yourself, the Excise will surely find you out. The fines are very heavy, and the prisons alas unlicensed."

In the foreword to the 1995 reprint, Adam's nephew Bill Bergius wrote:

> *"A sense of humour is one of the most precious gifts to man. Combined with an allegorical tale, it makes for a story that holds up in the memory and is fun to explore over and over again. Such was the achievement and originality of the creators of* Make Your Own Scotch Whisky. *Adam wrote the text to fill in the long flight home from Australia. As a master of the understatement, the author unfolds the magic of the process in crafting Scotch malt whisky by referring to things that touch our everyday Scottish lives. Combine this with Emett's inventive depictions and you have the imagery of the Scotch production process that is inimitable, sets the imagination alight and the lips smiling. Read on and take time to enjoy yourself."*

Apart from copies of *Make Your Own Scotch Whisky,* some of the original artwork for the promotional campaign remains, including a drawing of a lady with shopping. *Make Your Own Scotch Whisky* has been translated into nine languages and has sold over 7 million copies. It continues to be sold today and to make readers of all ages laugh. It makes the process of making whisky seem easy, but when you reread it you realize that it is only a dream and that in reality it is extremely hard … and expensive!

(Frederick) Rowland Emett OBE was born in 1906 and died in 1990. After leaving school he went to Birmingham School of Arts and Crafts, training to become a landscape painter. In 1931 his picture entitled *Cornish Harbour* was hung at the Royal Academy. In the 1930s he worked for advertising agencies until the Second World War intervened. During the war he started drawing cartoons and *Punch* accepted his first in 1939. By the end of the Second World War he had become a household name, especially following the creation of his cartoon "Nellie the Locomotive". In 1967 he was asked by United Artists to create a collection of machines for the film *Chitty Chitty Bang Bang*, including a car that could fly.

Adam Bergius put pen to paper again in 1974 when he created a fairy tale of the story of Teacher's Highland Cream in Brazil, revolving around the general manager Mr Guthrie. The aim of the book was to emphasize the fact that Brazilian customers were undoubtedly getting the genuine article, as Teacher's had started bottling in Brazil.

The end of an era was marked in 1960 with the closure of the dram shops. Jack House reported the following in the *Evening Times* of Friday 4 November 1960:

The automated bottling hall and bottle washer in the store and blended warehouse in King Street, occupied by Wᴹ Teacher & Sons 1898 to 1961.

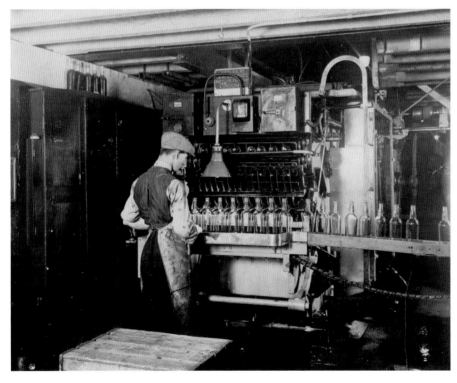

"A famous shop name disappears from the streets of Glasgow this weekend. It's the simple name of William Teacher and it has been painted over dark green pubs for 130 years. Teacher's pubs have been famous all that time for iron discipline – no drunkenness, no smoking, until that rule was relaxed for customers, but not for barmen, about 1922, and wee tables so that the customers would not sit around wasting their time in a frivolous manner. Indeed, the Teacher family, over these 130 years, have run what might be called Calvinistic pubs. And yet they have always done well. That may be because more Calvinists drink than we suspect. Or it may be that the original William Teacher's ideas were right. Or it may even be that Teacher's were selling something that the public must have, even if they had to deny themselves a cigarette and the scarlet leather and chromium amenities that are nowadays taken for granted."

The closing of the dram shops saw a shift in the company's strategy. The need to promote the company to new markets, including other licensed premises, meant increased marketing and advertising activity. The decision was made to move from King Street, which had served the company well for over 50 years as a bottling, warehousing, packaging and despatch depot.

In 1962 the company relocated to new purpose-built premises at Craigpark, Springburn, which opened on 21 March. The building and development of Craigpark was masterminded by Walter Andrew Bergius, who brought his engineering and distilling skills to the project. The plant took five years to construct and covered an area of 23,225 sq m (250,000 sq ft). Teacher's were able to blend, bottle and distribute all under one roof. For some, the decision to leave King Street with its unique layout under the arches of St Enoch Station must have been a hard one after so long. By the time Craigpark opened, the company was already exporting to over 150 countries.

In *The Spirit of Glasgow*, Edward Chisnall describes how Donald Campbell spent 42 years working at King Street starting work as a bottle-washer, becoming *'bond manager at King Street and later as superintendent at the new Craigpark complex. When Donald joined a team of some twenty men and boys in 1919 his first job was to wash bottles, making use of two large wooden tubs each holding about ten dozen bottles, closely packed. The bottling store at King Street was controlled by the august presence of Mr Ede, the Excise officer. Filling was done by one man, the stoppers were knocked in by another, and a third labelled the bottles and placed the precious items in boxes and crates. Output was in the region of sixty dozen or 720 bottles an hour. King Street really began to expand in 1924 with a boom in exports, and the new bottling hall trebled in size and covered 5,460 square feet, the vat capacity increased from 5,000 to 7,000 gallons, but washing was still done by hand. Mechanisation arrived in the world of traditional distilling in 1927 in the shape of a Dumore washing machine, Blair fillers, enormous Seitz Filters, and two mechanical Melvin bottling lines.'*

WHISKY TASTINGS, COLOUR ADVERTISING AND ANOTHER ADAM GOES TRAVELLING

The company introduced Whisky Tastings at St Enoch Square in the late 1960s and afterwards guests were given a copy of the leaflet "You have just attended a Whisky Tasting". It seems that Teacher's were the very first to introduce tastings to their visitors and they conducted the first public whisky tastings to André Simon's Wine and Food Society at the Waldorf Astoria in 1973.

Teacher's started producing more advertisements in colour in 1962. For the previous 50 years, with a few exceptions, Teacher's advertising had been in black and white. For the

USA there was a series based on the theme that things " … have changed since 1830, but the good taste of Teacher's never changes".

In the USA, and indeed the world, 1963 is remembered as the year John F. Kennedy (1917–63) was killed, allegedly by Lee Harvey Oswald. Kennedy was the first Roman Catholic President of the United States and one of its most charismatic leaders. He opposed racial discrimination and his short presidency gave Americans a sense of purpose in the new technological age.

Incidentally, the firm of Wm Teacher & Sons spanned the assassinations of four American Presidents. First was Abraham Lincoln who was killed by John Wilkes Booth in 1865, then James Garfield by Charles J. Guiteau in 1881 and William McKinley by Leon Czolgosz in 1901 and finally Kennedy in 1963.

In September 1964 Adam Bergius set off on a world tour that was to last until the end of November. Unlike his predecessor and namesake, Adam Teacher, he travelled in far more comfortable surroundings and without a full arsenal of weaponry. Adam, too, kept a diary of events, noting advertising and publicity material he saw and some of the problems encountered by overseas agents.

This tour should be seen in the context of the 1960s when overseas sales trips were uncommon. Companies conducted their export business principally by mail, telegram or telex. Telephone calls were rare and company directors would assemble in the same room to conduct conversations with overseas markets. It is hard to imagine how difficult it was to deal with overseas markets in today's world of instant communications using e-mail and mobile telephones. (I can still remember the excitement felt in my own office in 1968 when our Japanese agent came to visit, as up until then we had merely corresponded with him.)

Here are a few extracts from Adam's diary:

> *"Tuesday 29 September: In India. Unfortunately the day I was here, being a Tuesday, was one of prohibition, but with paying a premium, I managed to get a bottle of Dewars, which was in a terrible condition – dirty and scruffy … there were no whisky advertisements outside, that could be seen, to suggest Scotch whisky in any way."*

Nothing changes – members of Teacher's are still out and about looking critically at their own, and others, labelling standards.

> *"Wednesday 30th September: At Bangkok. Mr Khamkong Buahpetchra commonly known as Mr Khamkong was Teacher's agent in Thailand. Mr Khamkong complained about the lack of advertising material apart from a few pencils. He then went on to describe the way business was run in Thailand."*

Adam's diaries continue:

"Last year Khamkong's turnover in Bangkok and Siam was around 350 cartons and, so far this year, it is 150, with the Christmas trade to follow. Mr Khamkong stated that the young people in his territory were taking more to Scotch whisky than formerly, and it was very likely they would take more of it. There were no signs, billposts, etc., for Scotch whisky, that I could see. Mr Khamkong's wife has a sort of high-class draper-cum-souvenir shop below Mr Khamkong's office, and apparently she does very well. In the window of this shop was displayed HIGHLAND CREAM, Mateus Rose wine, of which they sell 400 cases per year, Lowenbrau beer, sales amounting to 700 cases per month, a few Marie Brizard liqueurs, of which they sell very little, and Kent and Windsor cigarettes … Mr Khamkong explained at length how the goods went into the black market at Laos, going under bond from Mr Khamkong's bonded store. Furthermore, goods go from the bond to Seato and UN, but very little of this goes to the black markets. The wholesale price to a merchant in Bangkok as a black-market carton of whisky is 900/1200 ticals per case, whereas, when Mr Khamkong clears in the proper way, he has to charge 1850 ticals per case."

In Tokyo Adam visited Sony Radio, Canon Camera and the Suntory Bottling Warehouse:

"Tuesday 6 October: At the Suntory Bottling Warehouse, we saw a remarkable film of the whisky distillery, situated about 500 miles distant in the south, and Mr Bergius has never seen anything so close to Ardmore, even a Scotch Whisky Distillery, as what was seen on the film. The arrangements, colour, shapes of all vessels, apart from the stills which were more of the Irish type, i.e. Saladin Maltings, steeps, conveyors, ploughs for the Saladin Boxes, grinding machines, and shape of the wash-back house, were all practically identical, even to the colour scheme. The mash tun was a little different, being a covered vessel, and the hot water is swirled into the mash tun, together with the grain entering at a separate point, and this is more or less continuous to take the place of the raking. Such must damage the grain, for to produce such motions it would require a severely working pump, which was not seen. They explained on the film that they get peat for the making of their Japanese whisky from Scotland, a point which has to be verified. Mr Bergius rather thinks it would be Irish. The standard of coopering really was amazing. Wood is obtained locally, and it seemed beautiful material. It would be worth our while to enquire, should wood become very difficult. In short, the excellence of the Japanese article would be as a result of the ability of the Japanese worker, rather than good working conditions, or even beautifully organised factories, together with extra-fine machinery. Whilst we saw the bottling arrangements at a distance through a glass window from a gallery like what we have at Craigpark, only much larger, it was seen that they have a very clever sighting machine, which should be followed up, to take the place of the Chelle machines in due course."

Adam did, however, encounter some difficulties, such as when he arrived on 10 October at Manila airport:

> *"Mr Real was not there at the airport to meet us, and the officials were very alarmed. They shut us into a private room to wait for Mr Real, and he did not turn up for something like one and a half hours, which was quite a wait. He had made a mistake with our aeroplane, although Mr Bergius had telegraphed him twice from Tokyo to advise arrival. It is to be feared that he is rather slack."*

The visit to Sydney was more successful, where Mr Halstead and the firm of Tucker's gave him a much warmer welcome. Tucker's are still Teacher's agents for Australia today:

> *"Went to see the bottling carried out in Tucker's warehouse. They have an Australian washing machine run on cold water, no heated water of any kind, and upstairs an Albro Filling Machine, Flower Stoppering Machine, and a World Labeller fitted up on a very simple belt conveyor. To finish off, bottles were wiped clean by hand, the rate of which is approximately 100/110 dozen per hour. The carton they have made in Australia is similar to ours, but the TEACHER face was very unpleasant. Mr Bergius sent a cable to Glasgow for a copy of the original TEACHER face."*

Squashed Bottle Ashtray. Produced in the early 1960s.

Supplies of advertising material also did not appear to be forthcoming in Australia:

> *"Mr Bergius asked Mr Halstead regarding advertising material received, and he said only drip mats and* Make Your Own Scotch Whisky *booklets were to hand. He stated that 250 cartons with 2 doz water siphons and 300 cartons with 1 doz of the squashed bottle ashtrays had not come to hand, although the same had been ordered way back in April.*

> *"Complimentary buffet cocktail party held by the Wine & Spirit Association … When the reply to the toast was made, great emphasis was put on the 'Fifty-Fifty with Water'."*

After a trip to New Zealand the business side of the trip ends, and references are made to Tahiti, Jamaica, Nassau (where Highland Cream was seen) and then *"on board the ship Ruahine it was noted that at least 90 per cent of our labels, back and front, were coming off and a letter was addressed to Mr Robert Dunlop of the fact, asking every attention to be carried out."*

A NEW JIGGER CAP FOR THE 1960S, THE BLACK ATHLETE

It is quite hard to see William Teacher really at home in the Swinging '60s, although with his forward thinking maybe he would have been able to understand the exhilaration and liberation experienced by young people at the time. In the UK it was a period of full employment and the musical revolution which had started in the USA with Chubby Checker, James Brown and Chuck Berry was re-exported by the Beatles (performing from 1961–70) with their mop-head haircuts and catchy tunes: *Please, Please Me*, *She Loves You* and *All You Need is Love*. Am not sure I can see him dancing to *Sgt Pepper's Lonely Hearts Club Band* or listening to the Rolling Stones, but perhaps I am wrong!

In 1967 Teacher's made a radical change to its bottle design by introducing a new oval-shaped bottle and, instead of the "Bury the Corkscrew" stopper, a new jigger cap. The jigger cap incorporated a screw-top which also acted as a measure. The gold colour of the cap was chosen by the chairman, Ronald Teacher. The unique styling of the cap with its own label was to be yet another innovation from Teacher's and remained in use until 1987. The new bottle design was launched at Expo 67 in Montreal where it received a design award. The label still resembled the 1913 version with black and gold lettering on a cream background, but the logo and typeface were bolder.

In 1968 further improvements were made to Craigpark with the installation of a demountable tank system with a 18,000 litre (4,000 gallon) stainless-steel tank. Similar

The water campaign was successful in both the UK and US markets. The igloo dates from 1966.

equipment was installed at Ardmore in 1969 and at Glendronach. In addition the company built the first duty-free warehouse in Scotland at Murano Street, Maryhill with automated bottling and a packaging line. With 5,200 sq m (56,000 sq ft) there was stacking space for 220,000 cartons. Production increased by over 300 per cent within 18 months and Teacher's coopers not only supplied the needs of Ardmore and Glendronach, but also other whisky companies.

Another year when Teacher's proved that they were not afraid to be different was 1970. In July 1968, Chairman Ronald McNairn Teacher warned shareholders that the company could not continue to absorb rising costs without seriously jeopardising export efforts. He said that, when the time came, home trade prices would have to increase. The company reached agreement with the Ministry of Agriculture, Fisheries and Food on 12 March 1970 and it was announced that the price of Teacher's would be increased by 2s. 6d. a bottle. This was a very brave move, as the market leader, Distillers Company Limited, had not raised its prices and it could be argued that Teacher's would lose out by doing so. Distillers did not in fact follow suit until September 1970 after continued pressure from its shareholders. The contribution made to Teacher's by Ronald McNairn Teacher should not be underestimated. He was chairman for over 20 years and he led the company through troubled times to success.

An article in *The Glasgow Herald* of 30 April 1970, entitled "Men who blend success at home and abroad" described the increase as follows:

"For nearly 150 years the firm of Wm Teacher and Sons Ltd have been pacemakers in the whisky business. Only a few weeks ago this pioneering instinct was displayed again in their decision to move towards a more realistic price for Scotch whisky on the home market. This step, soon followed by other independent distillers, would have had the approval of the founder of the firm, the first William Teacher, who was born midway

Herb Douglas, Schieffelin & Co with Marcia McBrown, who featured in Teacher's advertising, and Jesse Owen at the launch of *The Black Athlete*.

in history between the battles of Trafalgar and Waterloo. Although his enterprise was confined to trade in the United Kingdom, with no thoughts of the vast export market to come, he was a firm believer in two guiding principles – getting a fair price for good value, and maintaining quality.

"Teacher's – their head offices are now in St Enoch Square – have travelled a long and hard road since those peaceful days when William Teacher's string of retail shops in the cobbled streets of old Glasgow sold whisky across the counter at 2s. 6d. a bottle or 3d. a dram. But his descendants and their fellow directors on the present board, controlling the fortunes of what is now a great company spreading its tentacles over the whole whisky-drinking world, have remained faithful to these and other standards of their autocratic and forthright ancestor.

"To look towards the next move, or the next move but one, has always been characteristic of Teacher policy. The founder was forward looking when he planned each addition to his chain of dram shops, when he started his wholesale business of blending whiskies in bulk to suit the needs of individual customers and when he realized the wisdom of trusting his palate, and those of his sons William Teacher (Junior) and Adam Teacher, in the evolution of the blend that eventually became Highland Cream."

"*The Black Athlete* produced through a grant from Teacher's Scotch" is the headline on a news release from Schieffelin's public relations department, heralding the world première of the film in New York on 13 April 1971:

"The 37-minute film, narrated by Jesse Owens, begins with his spectacular performance in Berlin in the 1936 Olympic Games. The Black Athlete is not meant to be a 'message' film, but instead a primer of what has happened to the black American in the world of sports, and how he has changed the face of sports for all time. The Black Athlete was made possible by a grant from Wm Teacher & Sons, Ltd, Glasgow, Scotland. It was written, directed and produced by Bud Greenspan, a well-known sports film specialist."

(Bud Greenspan worked with Jesse Owens on *Return to Berlin*, the award-winning documentary of his career.)

The release went on to say that, *"Schieffelin & Co, sole US distributors for Teacher's Scotch will use the film through its national sales force for group showings across the country. Special premières will also be held in Chicago, Los Angeles and Atlanta during the month of May."* Herb Douglas, Vice President for National Special Markets, Schieffelin & Co, was the link with Jesse Owens. He and Jesse were close personal friends and Herb had won an Olympic bronze medal for the US track team in the 1948 Olympic Games in London.

ONE MILLION CASES AND "PICK UP A TEACHER"

The year of 1972 was a memorable one for Wm Teacher & Sons, for on 6 December Teacher's sales in the UK exceeded 1,000,000 cases: *"This was the first time that this magic figure had been surpassed in a calendar year and so, to mark this milestone in the company's history, the millionth case was set aside for special treatment."* As part of the celebrations Teacher's donated items including a solid-gold jigger cap and a commemorative bottle of Teacher's Highland Cream to the Licensed Victuallers' National Homes Prize draw. After four draws at major functions throughout 1973 the overall winner in October was Mr T. R. Blakeney of the King's Arms, Kennington Lane, London SE11. Teacher's flew Mr Blakeney up to the Glasgow head office for lunch with the Directors and to be presented with his prize.

Mr Blakeney was at the time Vice-Chairman and Treasurer of the South London Victualler's and as part of his prize he also won the right to claim a Teacher's Director as "Banquet Guest of the Evening" at their annual dinner on 15 May 1974. Ronnie Anderson, at the time Senior Sales Director at Wm Teacher & Sons, was the guest of honour. He said,

1973 Mr Blakeney receives his solid-gold jigger cap from Adam K. Bergius (Chairman of the company at the time).

In a Class by Itself
since the 1830s.
USA Campaign
circa 1962.

Ships have changed since 1830 but the good taste of TEACHER'S never changes!

In a class by itself since 1830

TEACHER'S
HIGHLAND CREAM Scotch Whisky

86 PROOF · Blended Scotch Whisky · Schieffelin & Co., New York

Ad No. 57-TCH-415 A

"It is a great pleasure for me to be here chairing the South London Licensed Victuallers and Beer Sellers Charitable Association, and I am very conscious of the fact that I am making history by doing so. This is, in fact, the first time my company has taken the Chair at an LVA function in England. I hasten to add this is not because we don't like English LVAs, on the contrary, we love them, particularly as their members have been a major factor in our breaking through the millionth case barrier, as it has been called."

Ronnie's speech goes on to say that he realizes that they are not *"unique in this achievement, but we felt it was worthwhile marking this milestone in the company's history in a special way"*, so clearly Teacher's were not the first. But for one of the few remaining independents it was certainly a notable milestone in the company's development.

An article appeared in *The Glasgow Herald* on 12 March 1975 in a special feature entitled "Pacemaker", following companies who had made a significant contribution to the local economy. This coincided with Teacher's 145th anniversary and also 100 years at their head offices in St Enoch Square, Glasgow. At the time there were five family members on the board: Adam Bergius was Chairman, George Teacher Dunlop was Managing Director, Ronnie Anderson was Senior Sales Director, Bill Bergius was Sales Director and Robert Dunlop Senior was Production Director.

Bill Bergius joined the company in 1970, having served with 21 SAS (Special Air Service) in London and then worked for United States Lines in Glasgow. He became a member of the Teacher's board in 1975 and 30 years later is still a Director of the company.

During the late 1960s and 1970s Teacher's started picking up themes from early advertising and looked at using a play on the word "Teacher". This was a bolder campaign using "Teacher Girls" to promote the brand in cap and gown. Some of the captions were quite saucy, for example "Pick up a Teacher". We wonder whether William Teacher would have approved! This slogan appeared on beer mats, shoe-shine cloths and other items. The promotional booklet, from which some of the accompanying photographs are produced, includes bottles with the words "Bottled in Scotland" in red for the export market and 12-year old bottles of Teacher's Royal Highland Deluxe Blended Scotch Whisky. This campaign was closely followed by "In a Class of its Own", which was used throughout the 1970s and into the 1980s.

This was a busy period for American advertising, with key personalities such as Peter Townsend, Redd Foxx, Sammy Davis Junior and David Frost endorsing Teacher's whisky. Not part of this particular series and certainly the longest featuring a celebrity in terms of copy was one of Groucho Marx, produced from 1972–75. The double-page spread advertisement was headed "Whenever I think of Scotch, I recall the immortal words of my brother Harpo."

I told the scotch people
I don't drink any more. Then again, I don't
drink any less, either.

BY REDD FOXX

D ON'T GET THE impression that I'm a heavy drinker. I only weigh 150 pounds.

Talking about drinking is part of my nightclub act. It's probably the only part of my nightclub act I can talk about in print.

But, seriously, there's a Redd Foxx nobody knows. And I wish they'd find him because he's been signing my name to a lot of checks.

The thing is that underneath it all, I'm really a clean-living family man. Well, at least, a family man.

And speaking of my family, my great grandfather, Redd Foxx, the First, was the first Black political candidate in the State of Mississippi. He ran for the border and made it. And the reason he ran for the border, he said, was that the people were very clannish. He didn't mind them having hang ups, he just didn't want to be one of their hang ups.

But, I have to say, my favorite was my Uncle Nedd Foxx, the First. He was a Labor Union man. Till the day he died. In fact, he died because he was a Union man. You see, he was in this boat that sank in the middle of the Atlantic. About 12 hours from shore. Of course, he wouldn't swim any more than eight hours. After all, he wasn't getting time and a half. I admire a man who stands up for his principles. Or, in this case, goes under for them.

It was this same Uncle who gave me three pieces of advice I'll never forget.

"Marry an ugly woman," he said, "when she leaves you'll be happy."

(I did, but I'm getting tired of waiting for her to leave.)

He also said, "If you want to keep your teeth in good condition, brush them after every meal and mind your own business."

And the last thing he said...well... it slips my mind.

But with all his memorable advice, look at where Uncle Nedd ended up. In the drink.

Which brings me to the subject in hand. The drink.

When I started out as an entertainer, I used to try to make a big splash. Drove a flashy car, drank the biggest name booze.

You can understand why. I mean, I had plenty to make up for. When I was a kid, my family was so poor, I had to wear my brother's hand-me-downs at the same time he was wearing them. Things got kind of embarrassing for me when he left home.

But then came the Depression. It was a blessing for us.

So you can understand why I started showing some flash the minute I started getting some cash.

But, these days, while I still drive a nice car, I drink for my sake, not somebody else's. So I drink Teacher's. Looking good just isn't as important to me as drinking good. And drinking Teacher's is drinking good. On the rocks, on a stool, wherever.

Well, I hope it doesn't take my kids as long to grow up as it took me.

And speaking of kids, isn't it great to watch as those precious things grow from little kernels into big nuts. Except, like any nuts, to get the most out of them, they occasionally have to be cracked. But my oldest kid is too big for me to hit. He's 6' 3". So I let my wife take care of him. She's 6' 4".

Well, this has been fun, but I have to stop now. It's time for my morning eggs and toast. I always like my eggs scrambled and my toast on the rocks.

In the Battle of Britain, there were two things that kept us going. Spirit and spirits.

BY PETER TOWNSEND

Don't get me wrong. We weren't exactly a fly-by-night group of high livers. But, while we fighter pilots were hardened professionals in the air, on the ground we were a pretty happy-go-lucky lot.

We used to say our job was kind of sporting. Maybe it was. But it was a highly dangerous sport in which you had to be right on the ball.

The thing is, though, when you have to work that hard, it sometimes helps to play hard, too. You're like a complicated piece of machinery that occasionally has to be oiled. So off days were party days for us. Dedicated to getting oiled.

Often, the parties were quite impromptu. One pilot bailed out one evening after a furious combat only to land in the garden of a country house where the guests were just arriving for drinks. But those were times when no one frowned on such undignified gate crashing. Or roof crashing. In fact, when the pilot finally left, they invited him to drop in anytime he was in the neighborhood.

I too got involved in one of these spur-of-the-moment parties. The main difference, though, was that I bailed out at 6:30 A.M. in the drink. Hauled aboard a trawler, I was immediately handed a drink to warm me up. But the party was just getting warmed up. For, when a few hours later, the ship docked alongside three others, glasses were raised on each to the survivor. That was me. Glasses were then raised again. And again. Until I wasn't sure I was the survivor.

To tell you the truth, you never knew in those stirring and uncertain times with whom you might be having a "noggin." Early one afternoon after a particularly unpleasant mix up with some Messerschmitts I found myself flat on my backside in a Kentish wood.

It wasn't long, however, before I found myself on my backside on a soft chair in a Kentish pub. A burly countryman had picked me up and drove me at break-neck speed to the "local." We made it just before closing time. And I think we stayed till just before opening time.

And while the battle continued to rage overhead, we continued raising glasses overhead to the damnation of our enemy, who, at the moment were getting a somewhat fiery reception.

But, while there were things you couldn't be certain of, there were also things you could be certain of.

Like what you'd get when someone would buy a whisky for you.

For, in England, then as now, when you say whisky, you mean scotch. And the scotch you're likely to get is Teacher's.

So there's been a lot of Teacher's under the bridge.

Which was all well and good. I mean when they haul you out of the water at 6:30 in the morning, you'll drink anything, so it might as well be something good.

And, when people, out of the goodness of their hearts offer you a drink, you can't really refuse.

So, again, it's a good thing the English know their scotch.

Those were times when it was tough to keep a stiff upper lip. But just as it seemed that our spirits were at their lowest we'd always get a fresh influx of spirits from somewhere or other. Usually, it was Teacher's. You might say it was one of the things that kept us flying.

Whenever I think of Scotch, I recall the immortal words of my brother Harpo.

BY GROUCHO MARX

Harpo was a man of very few words, except when it came to scotch, horses and ladies.

Actually, scotch ran a poor third. Which wasn't easy considering the way his horses ran.

And the way his horses ran could be summed up in a word.

Last.

He once had a horse who finished ahead of the winner of the 1942 Kentucky Derby.

Unfortunately, the horse started running in the 1941 Derby.

And as far as the ladies go, Harpo's ladies always went.

As a matter of fact, they went a lot faster than his horses. Although his horses were a lot prettier.

But that's a horse of a different color.

Anyway, back to the subject at hand. What was it again? Oh, yeah, scotch.

When it came to scotch, Harpo's words were memorable.

Unfortunately, I forget them.

I remember the thought behind them, however.

The thought was that Harpo appreciated good scotch. Especially one kind of scotch. I know this because one morning I found my liquor cabinet broken into. All the scotch was opened and apparently samples were taken of each bottle. Except in the case of Teacher's Scotch where the case was taken.

I immediately put on my Sherlock Holmes hat, replaced my cigar with a pipe and looked for my thinking cap, but I couldn't find it.

"The Case of the Missing Case," I called it.

Harpo was my number one suspect. He was also my number two and my number three suspect.

The night before I had heard a honking sound in my living room. At first I thought it was a car looking for a parking space in my apartment. (That used to happen a lot until I had parking meters installed.) Little did I know, however, that it was my brother committing one of the most unbrotherly acts since the Andrews Sisters.

So I threw a mackinaw over my Dr. Denton's and dashed off to Harpo's. I must have cut quite a dashing figure.

When I arrived at Harpo's house, there, big as life, were my bottles of Teacher's.

"Why, Harpo?" I asked, lighting my cigar and putting it out on the rug, the one on the floor.

Harpo answered with a honk that was worth a thousand words.

I understood them immediately.

What it boiled down to was that Teacher's tasted better to him than any of the other scotches I had.

I agreed with that. It also tasted better to me. That's probably why we're brothers. After all, scotch is thicker than water.

And, on the subject of brothers, Harpo said he knew enough about scotch to know that Teacher's wasn't one of those scotches everybody and his brother drinks.

I told him he was doing his best to change that.

Then I asked him how he knew that anyway.

Well, to make a long story longer, it seems that he had gone through Gummo's liquor cabinet, too. As well as Zeppo's and Chico's. Before he went through mine. And he said that I had the best taste.

I said, "That's all very interesting, Harpo, but now it's time to play 'You Bet Your Life.' And give me a finger of my own scotch while you're at it."

To show me how generous he was he poured some scotch into a glass and put his whole hand into it. I'd had scotch and water, scotch and soda, but never scotch and hand. But then, Harpo's an old hand at serving scotch. At the risk of beating a hand to death, let me continue. Where was I . . .

At this point I told Harpo I didn't want to hear any more horns.

He honked.

I said, "Say it with strings."

So he grabbed his harp and proceeded to play me to sleep. I snored in accompaniment.

It was while I was sleeping that he uttered those now immortal words. You know the words I mean. At least I hope you do. Cause you couldn't expect me to remember the words somebody said to me while I was sleeping.

But, after all, why harp on that.

Teacher's
A Lesson in
Scotch

1.   THE ITALIAN TEACHER

When not in Rome, do as the
Romans do.

3 ounces Teacher's Highland Cream
1 ounce Cinzano Sweet Vermouth
1 dash Angostura bitters
Slice of Orange
Serve over the rocks.

4. THE ENGLISH TEACHER

The English reveal the reason they are
able to go out in the midday snow,
as well as the midday sun.

1 ounce Teacher's Highland Cream
4 ounces hot (or cold) strong Tetley tea
Slice of lemon

Serve piping hot or over the rocks,
depending on external temperature.

8. THE CHRISTMAS TEACHER

A great way to celebrate Christmas, the world over.

1 bottle (750 ml.) Teacher's Highland Cream
2 quarts prepared eggnog
½ pint heavy cream
Nutmeg
Combine Teacher's and eggnog in 3-quart punch bowl and refrigerate at least 2 hours. Just before serving, stir thoroughly. Beat cream until stiff and ladle onto surface of eggnog. Sprinkle liberally with nutmeg. Serves 24.

The teaching theme was also picked up by Schieffelin in the USA who launched a campaign in 1979 "A Lesson in Scotch". The campaign also included the slogan "No Scotch improves the flavour of water like Teacher's". A booklet "Teacher's International Lessons in Scotch" gave recipes for cocktails such as The Italian Teacher, The Scottish Teacher and The Naked Teacher:

> "… with a body like Teacher's Highland Cream, there's nothing to be embarrassed about. Wherever you are, 4 ounces Teacher's Highland Cream, a twist of lemon peel, and serve on the rocks."

ESTD · W^M TEACHER & SONS · GLASGOW · 1830

TAKEOVERS, "A WELCOME AWAITING" AND TEACHER'S 60

By the end of the 1970s whisky production had been affected by a general slump because of the oil crisis. Additionally, the US, which had long been a key market for whisky companies, suffered a recession prompted by a downturn in the economy following the end of the Vietnam War. The deluxe brands fared better and interest in single malts was just starting to grow. Single malt distilleries were improving the way they operated and increasing the quality and quantity of their whiskies.

In 1976 Adam Bergius followed in his father William Manera's footsteps by initiating a meeting with Allied Brewers to avoid the possibility of Teacher's becoming the subject of a hostile takeover. The year before the company had celebrated its 145th anniversary, but the need to raise additional capital to maintain growth and meet the high taxation on UK whisky sales had meant that the shareholding had to be increased. The Teacher family interests were much reduced and the support of a larger organisation seemed essential. Within three days an agreement had been reached, with Adam confident that Allied would honour the Teacher ethos and ensure that the brands would continue to grow.

Adam Bergius, like his father, grandfather and great-grandfather, is a man of great personality and drive. It would be impossible to write about the Teacher family without including a little more about Adam. An article in the *Helensburgh Advertiser*, on 23 February 1979 was headlined, "Once a war hero in midget submarines, now he is … The whisky baron, 1979". Journalist Dorothy Fenwick writes of Adam:

> *"To a stranger Adam Bergius may seem a shy man, but that shyness masks the courage, ability and determination which has made him a Second World War hero, taken him to the top in a cut-throat industrial scene, and enabled him to mastermind the successful start of Helensburgh's new Lomond School as the first chairman of the board of governors."*

In the interview, Adam continues in his own words. "I joined the company after leaving the Royal Navy at the end of the war [Second World War] and in fact I really wanted to be a farmer and had read a great deal about agriculture during the war years. But my brother Cecil was killed during the war and after it ended I began working in the company at the bottom and really didn't like the work for the first few years. Then they made me export director which I enjoyed, and this was a side of the company which was to expand greatly over the succeeding years."

He joined the Royal Navy as an ordinary seaman at the age of 17 in 1944 and served as a submariner commanding a midget four-man submarine. Like all members of the Teacher/ Bergius family, Adam retains a love of the sea and became the first Commodore of

Helensburgh Sailing Club. Now in his 80s, he continues to cruise on his *Annie*, a 30ft gaff-rigged yacht.

In 1979 Margaret Thatcher became the first woman to lead a Western democracy. Her leadership of the country from 1979–90 was to have a huge effect on the UK economy. The 1980s were booming and the pre-eminence of London as a financial centre was re-established, but the Trade Unions suffered and the manufacturing base declined. A key element of Mrs Thatcher's tenure was her relationship with Ronald Reagan, who was President of the USA from 1981–88. Together they forged closer links, and these are still in place today.

The early 1980s were interesting times for all whisky companies, as the continuing drive to increase production during the previous two decades meant that supplies far exceeded orders from the marketplace. In the UK the supermarkets started to flex their muscles and not only demanded good-quality whiskies at reduced prices but introduced their "own brands". This, combined with an ever-increasing tax burden, led many whisky companies to retrench and this led to the closure of a large number of distilleries. Teacher's, with only Ardmore and Glendronach at the time, were better placed than others to weather the storm.

"IT SAVES MR FAGAN THE TROUBLE OF CLIMBING FIVE FLIGHTS OF STAIRS!"

Fagan laughs and laughs

IT wasn't even good wine. And Michael Fagan was a whisky drinker, Teacher's if he had a choice.

So when he looked over the dock at the empty bottle standing up on the exhibit table he laughed his head off.

Fagan laughed and laughed. He laughed at everything, even when the judge called him an 'oddball'.

Number One Court, the Old Bailey, had seen some material laid out on the exhibit table: Knives and hatchets, jugs of poison, and all kinds of guns.

No case could be recalled when all the police put on as evidence was a bottle.

If he had got it out of a supermarket the whole thing would have been dealt with way down the line.

Fagan, of course, went over the railings into Buckingham Palace, climbed 51ft up drainpipes and over roofs and went into Room 108, The Post Room, and drank about two glassfulls from the neck out of a bottle sent to Prince Charles and the Princess of Wales to celebrate the forthcoming birth of Prince William.

The bottle came through the whole system of investigation and yesterday ended up empty between the Recorder of London, James Miskin, QC, and Michael Fagan, of several addresses.

It was turned around for everybody to see. California Reisling '81, beach party stuff.

Fagan in his red pullover and open-necked cream shirt sat back deeply in his chair in the dock and just got lost in the whole excitement of the story being told in court.

When they got to the bit where his steps were being traced from the street to The Post Room, Fagan, 30, bounced up and down urging them to go faster.

Fagan was a slight, little man with gangling hands. His brown hair tumbled back and his nose had a hump on it as though it had been broken sometime.

He talked at the speed of light with a Cockney accent.

It was like listening to a man speaking in ciphers.

How the Queen ever understood him only she knows.

His old mother Ivy Fagan was up in the gallery swaying and crying with her distress. But Fagan was horse riding in the dock and his curly hair flopped everywhere.

The jury switched from looking at Fagan to looking at the bottle. Then they went to Mrs Barbara Mills who prosecuted and up in the gallery to the Fagan family who were saying things towards the dock with their eyes and Mrs Fagan mouthed 'I love you' many times.

Mrs Mills opened a folder of 15 pictures—taken later—which showed just how Fagan made it to The Post Room.

It began at the Buckingham Gate side of the Palace, the left side if you look at it from the front.

Fagan went up over the railings and into Ambassador's Court, up some drain

Turn to Page 2, Col. 1

INSIDE: Weather 2, World Wide 4, Femail 12, 13, Diary 23, TV and Radio 26, 27, Prize Crossword, Motoring 34, Letters 36, City 38, 39

Michael Fagan achieved notoriety in the UK by gaining entry illegally to Buckingham Palace on 7 June 1982 and drinking a bottle of wine. After his trial on 23 September a report of the incident appeared in the *Daily Mail*. John Edward reported that Fagan didn't really like wine; he "was a whisky drinker, Teacher's if he had a choice." This prompted JAK, one of the UK's finest cartoonists, to show a picture of Her Majesty The Queen leaving a bottle of Teacher's on her doorstep and saying, "It saves Mr Fagan the trouble of climbing five flights of stairs!"

The UK Campaign "A Welcome Awaiting" was launched in 1982. This heralded the start of Teacher's biggest-ever advertising spend in one year – £1 million. A new roundel with a bottle of Teacher's and a glass, either held in someone's hand or on its own, was designed. This was used as part of an advertisement with the words "Est. 1830 Teacher's Highland Cream" or on its own with the words "Teacher's. A Welcome Awaiting". The full-colour pictures were some of the most evocative used by Teacher's throughout their history. They showed a shepherd, ploughman or fisherman returning home to a lighted window after a hard day's work.

The campaign continued with a £1 million spend for three years and ran in conjunction with trade advertising persuading on and off licences to order Teacher's with the slogan "There's no business like Teacher's". In 1983 the design team started looking at the front

label of the Teacher's Highland Cream bottle and this change was launched in 1984 to increase the impact of the brand.

As with all Teacher's initiatives, promotional and point-of-sale material accompanied "A Welcome Awaiting". The opportunity to win one of five holidays for two in the USA was offered to outlets stocking Teacher's Highland Cream on optic measure in a leaflet "Escape from Life Behind Bars". I am assured that there was no real link between the behind bars theme and San Francisco, the home of the infamous Alcatraz prison and one of the winning destinations!

Allied Brewers purchased United Rum Merchants in 1984 and they provided a new sales force with additional product lines, thus widening the appeal of the company to both the on and off trade.

Following increased production in 1970, by 1985 there was an excess of high-quality whisky in the industry, even the great single malts. Most companies decided to package it up and sell it cheap, but Teacher's were different and launched a superior Teacher's expression on the basis of while stocks last. Teacher's 60 was launched in Scotland in 1985. This contains at least 60 per cent pure malt whiskies and one of the key components is the company's own Glendronach, a distinctive Highland Whisky. The launch was so successful that the following year Teacher's 60 became available throughout the UK.

SUPPORTED BY MILLIONS.

Teacher's Highland Cream is one of the two best-selling brands of Scotch Whisky.

Support for Teacher's Highland Cream comes from millions of customers, and it is backed year in year out by consistent advertising support. £3 million in three years has been invested in the "Teacher's. A Welcome Awaiting" campaign.

So when you next order whisky, remember:

THERE'S NO BUSINESS LIKE TEACHER'S.

CLUB SECRETARY OCTOBER 1983

TEACHER'S 60 is guaranteed to contain at least
60% pure malt whiskies. Included in the make-up
of Teacher's 60 is The Glendronach Highland malt,
together with Speyside malts and carefully selected
grain whisky to balance the blend. The result is a
finished whisky of remarkable refinement with a full,
distinctive character and depth of flavour.

WHISKY FROM THE OLD SCHOOL

EXPANSION, THE GLENDRONACH SINGLE MALT AND THE EUROPEAN CITY OF CULTURE 1990

Allied Brewers went on the acquisition trail and in 1982 purchased Lyons, renaming the company Allied-Lyons, and then in 1987 Hiram Walker Gooderham & Worts of Canada. Hiram Walker started purchasing whisky companies in Scotland in the 1930s, following the end of Prohibition in the USA. They acquired Glenburgie distillery first, then others such as Glencadam, Ardbeg and Scapa and diversified into purchasing famous brands such as Ballantine's. These acquisitions meant that Teacher's

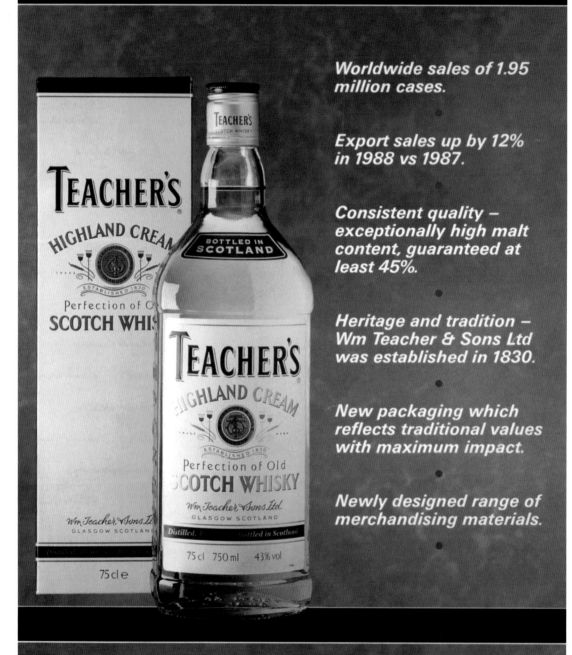

THE ON-GOING SUCCESS STORY

Worldwide sales of 1.95 million cases.

Export sales up by 12% in 1988 vs 1987.

Consistent quality – exceptionally high malt content, guaranteed at least 45%.

Heritage and tradition – Wm Teacher & Sons Ltd was established in 1830.

New packaging which reflects traditional values with maximum impact.

Newly designed range of merchandising materials.

had access to a wider range of single malts "in-house" and a larger international sales and marketing team. One thing, however, that the directors understood was that the Teacher's brand must never be compromised and that the original recipe is sacrosanct.

In 1987 Teacher's looked again at the bottle design. This was as a result of commercial pressure to replace the jigger cap with a more visible pilfer-proof closure. The new design featured many of the previous elements but the bottle itself changed with Teacher's embossed on both sides. The jigger cap was replaced by a standard screw-top.

In 1988 Allied Lyons formed a company called Allied Distillers Ltd to bring together the interests of their Scotch brands, Wm Teacher & Sons, Stewarts of Dundee and George Ballantine & Son.

Craigpark, the company's blending, bottling and distribution operation closed in 1988 and the activities moved to the under-used Ballantine's operation at Kilmalid, Dumbarton, close to the River Clyde. Incidentally, Dumbarton is a few miles down the river west of Glasgow – the company had almost retraced William's steps from Duntocher to Anderston 158 years ago. In 1989 Allied Distillers added to its malt portfolio with the purchase of Imperial and Glentauchers distilleries.

The Glendronach was experiencing a surge of interest, like all distilleries, in its single malt whisky. Teacher's had built up a superb inventory of Glendronach casks and the idea was conceived to launch two different versions. For the very first time consumers were able to purchase a Glendronach, which had been totally matured in old sherry casks and another, known as "Original", matured in a mix of sherry and bourbon casks. This idea was quickly adopted by other distillery companies, most notably Glenmorangie, who took the idea one step further and adapted their traditional maturation methods to create a range of finished malts. Both Glendronach labels feature a fine-line drawing of the distillery complete with the trees and the surrounding countryside. A new burgundy livery was introduced for its promotional material, together with the Glendronach Tartan in distinctive burgundy, green and yellow.

In 1988, the directors responsible for Teacher's Highland Cream started to look again at one of the company's key activities over the years – interest in and sponsorship of the Arts. They also knew that Glasgow had won the prestigious European Year of Culture Award 1990. Visitors would be coming to the city to see the artistic, architectural and design legacies of Glasgow's glorious past, as well as celebrating its regeneration and the young artists working today. The Teacher's building in St Enoch Square was to become the "Glasgow 1990 Press Centre" and thus a focus of interest.

Teacher's decided to replicate the idea of the collection built up by Adam Teacher in the 19th century when he supported modern Scottish artists. The decision was made that every artist had to be Scottish and to have superior quality and character, just like Teacher's

"The Whisky Taster," painted by James Knight, is in the Glen House at Teacher's Glendronach Distillery. The painting was presented to the company by Walter A. Bergius, a former Chairman.

Highland Cream. Some of the artists were already well recognized in the Scottish art world, but others were less well known.

Pictures and sculptures were purchased from, among others, Christine McArthur, Norman Kirkham, Duncan Shanks, John Cunningham and James Robertson. The choice of media was wider than in Adam's day and there are paintings using oil, pastel, watercolour and mixed media, as well as etchings and a bronze figure and wooden sculpture. After the European City of Culture the collection was moved to the Glendronach distillery where it can still be seen today.

During the Year of Culture Teacher's continued its support of the Glasgow Festival Strings and also sponsored Glasgow's Tramway Theatre's production by La Gran Scena Opera, a calendar for the Scottish National Orchestra and a drama series *The Bell in the Tree* on Radio Clyde, Glasgow's own radio station. The company also announced the funding of an Annual Art Travel Scholarship of £2,000. All a very fitting celebration, just over 100 years later, of the remarkable legacy made by Adam Teacher to the City of Glasgow.

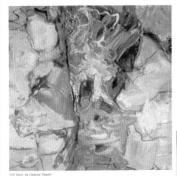

Fall Burst by Duncan Shanks

THE TEACHER'S ART COLLECTION AT GLENDRONACH

Bill Bergius and John Campbell collecting the Teacher's Art Collection

The Study at the Glen House, Glendronach

The Entrance Hall at the Glen House, Glendronach

Unexpected Visitor by Lesley Banks

The Dining Room at the Glen House, Glendronach

The Teacher's Distillery at Glendronach is the current home of the Art Collection and now, in the tranquil surroundings of the Glen House, company guests can view the Collection at their leisure.

The decision to establish a collection of contemporary Scottish Art was taken as part of Teacher's contribution to the year of celebration enjoyed by Glasgow when it was European City of Culture in 1990. From the outset, there were certain constraints that the company set for itself in the task of setting up the Collection. Every artist had to be Scottish, and every piece had to have superior quality and character. These three descriptions – Scottishness, quality and character, can of course be used to describe Teacher's Highland Cream itself.

Forty works of art have been brought together. Several of the artists, such as John Cunningham, Duncan Shanks, Lesley Banks and Christine McArthur, are well recognised in the Scottish art world as being at the forefront of contemporary Scottish activity. While some of the other artists are less well-known, each individual piece in the Collection is there on merit.

In common with other prominent Scottish firms, from time to time, Teacher's plays host to many visitors. Now, the presence of the Collection at Glendronach, a destination for our key guests, lets them feel more of the quality of Scotland. For these guests, the Teacher's Art Collection enhances the quality and heritage of Teacher's.

"WHISKY FROM THE OLD SCHOOL", TEACHER'S CITY SCRIBBLERS AND TEACHER'S SCRAMBLE

Teacher's Highland Cream had, for the past 18 years, been one of biggest users of posters in the UK. By 1988 it was the largest, and the new campaign launched in 1989 "Whisky from the Old School" focused on this media. The sales director at the time, Simon Sanders, who spearheaded the campaign, said, "We're putting our money where our mouth is – twice as much for Highland Cream compared with 1987, with a package of activities and advertising support that will have tremendous impact on the trade and consumers. The message is growth and we're confident of achieving it."

"Whisky from the Old School" in some ways harked back to the Teacher themes but with a different twist. No teachers in black gowns and mortarboards, simply blackboards with chalked messages such as "Favourite", and "Sips of the Best". The poster campaign continued into 1990 when £2.5 million was spent between March and December. For the Wimbledon Tennis Championships the blackboard read "Perfect for Singles and Doubles", and in response to Prime Minister Margaret Thatcher's firm approach one showed the message "There's No Alternative", and just in time for Christmas the slogan "Three Wise Men" appeared with three glasses of whisky in front of the board. 1991 saw "10/10 for flavour" and "Have an educated guess" added to the range of blackboard notes.

The Teacher's Girls, however, were back and they could be seen giving away prizes at race meetings, creating cocktails, offering celebrity authors such as John Mortimer a drink at the Teacher's Sunday Night Lecture at the Edinburgh Book Festival and supporting other promotional activity.

Something to raise your spirits.

It's traditional apparatus like this gleaming "spirit safe" that helps us take the utmost care of Teacher's whisky. It's true that all blended Scotch whiskies are made from two kinds of whisky. Malt and grain.

And we're proud that Teacher's Highland Cream has an exceptionally high malt content. Guaranteed at least 45% pure malt whiskies.

This is just one of the features which contributes to the unique character and full flavour of Teacher's Highland Cream.

WHISKY FROM THE OLD SCHOOL.

To lead the field, we harvest it.

On our Aberdeenshire estate we still sow and harvest our own barley, as we have done for years. It's a fraction of what we need, but it ensures we know good barley when we buy it.

We also maintain the long-standing tradition of including an exceptionally high proportion of pure malt whiskies in our blend.

This is just one of the reasons why Teacher's Highland Cream continues to be both full-flavoured and remarkably smooth.

WHISKY FROM THE OLD SCHOOL.

Arranged marriages in Scotland.

At Teacher's we never rush into "marriage". We've spent years getting to know Scotland's finest single malt and grain whiskies so that we can blend them together and allow them to "marry" into the perfect union known as Teacher's Highland Cream.

And of course, we include an exceptionally high proportion of pure malt whiskies in our blend, which helps ensure our unique character, full flavour and remarkable smoothness.

WHISKY FROM THE OLD SCHOOL.

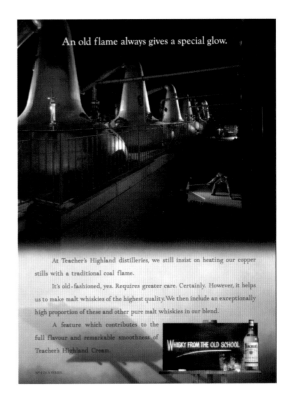

An old flame always gives a special glow.

At Teacher's Highland distilleries, we still insist on heating our copper stills with a traditional coal flame.

It's old-fashioned, yes. Requires greater care. Certainly. However, it helps us to make malt whiskies of the highest quality. We then include an exceptionally high proportion of these and other pure malt whiskies in our blend.

A feature which contributes to the full flavour and remarkable smoothness of Teacher's Highland Cream.

WHISKY FROM THE OLD SCHOOL.

In 1990 Allied Lyons were on the acquisition trail yet again with the purchase of Whitbread's Spirit Division. This meant that the company added Laphroaig and Tormore distilleries to its portfolio, as well as Black Bottle and Long John blended whiskies and, incidentally, another very traditional brand, Beefeater's Gin. Beefeater, which is the UK's leading gin distilled in London, was founded by James Burrough who was born in 1834 – he too was a legend in his lifetime, but that is another story.

The Teacher's City Scribblers Awards was devised to raise much-needed funds for Barts Hospital's City Life Saver Scheme. St Bartholomew's, or Barts as it is affectionately known, is the City of London's main hospital and also a leading centre of excellence for heart surgery. The Barts City Life Saver Scheme has successfully taught many thousands of City people to recognize the symptoms of a heart attack. The training course teaches basic cardiac life support, which is crucial if a victim is to stay alive until the ambulance arrives.

The competition ran for two years in 1989 and 1990. Entrants were asked to submit cartoons or limericks (a limerick is a form of comic verse of five lines, where the first, second and fifth should rhyme and also the third and fourth – not everyone got it right!). Many of the entries focused, quite naturally, on living and working in the City and problems associated with being a member of the European Community. Bill Bergius' cousin, Peter, working with Kleinwort Benson Securities, submitted a cartoon entry.

Sir Colin Marshall's entry, at the time Chief Executive of British Airways:

> *"An analyst living in Bow,*
> *Said 'Here is the one thing I know;*
> *My advice makes no sense*
> *But when traffic is dense*
> *It's faster by Tube to Heathrow.'"*

Malcolm Cleaves' entry, a London taxi driver (cabbie):

> *"Teacher's – the finest of brands*
> *London's cabbies – the best in the land*
> *Linked together at Barts*
> *Where we aim for the heart*
> *Once again saving lives, hand in hand."*

P. Bergius
Kleinwort Benson Securities Ltd.

Teacher's Pursuits was launched in 1990 and continued until 1993. This was a campaign focusing on a range of sports and leisure activities such as golf, fishing and racing, and trade competitions included prizes to The US Masters Golf and The Hong Kong Sevens Rugby.

And then there was the Teacher's Scramble, which was run in association with *Golf Monthly* magazine, and started at the beginning of 1990; 38,000 amateur golfers from 580 clubs and 18 teams of four, who had won the initial club competitions as well as 12 area finals met at Turnberry Hotel on Scotland's Ayrshire Coast to play for "William", the Teacher's Scramble Trophy. The winners were from Strabane Golf Club in Northern Ireland, closely followed by a team from Crook Golf Club, Co. Durham and Crail Golf Club, Fife. The second Teacher's Scramble attracted even more entries in 1991 with 930 clubs and 90,000 amateur golfers taking part. This year the final was at Dalmahoy and the winners were again from Northern Ireland, this time from Ardglass Golf Club.

SPORTS SPONSORSHIP, ALLIED DOMECQ, BRAZIL AND INDIA GROW

Teacher's also continued to sponsor other sports. The Scottish men's and women's curling teams went on to win the European Championship in 1989 sponsored by Teacher's and both teams reached the finals of the World Championship in 1990. The Teacher's Clydesdale Cricket Club reached the finals of the Scottish Cup in 1991. And for the more sedentary sportsmen and women, Teacher's sponsored the European Backgammon Championships in Deauville, France in 1989.

Rennie MacIntosh special bottling for Glasgow Year of Culture 1990.

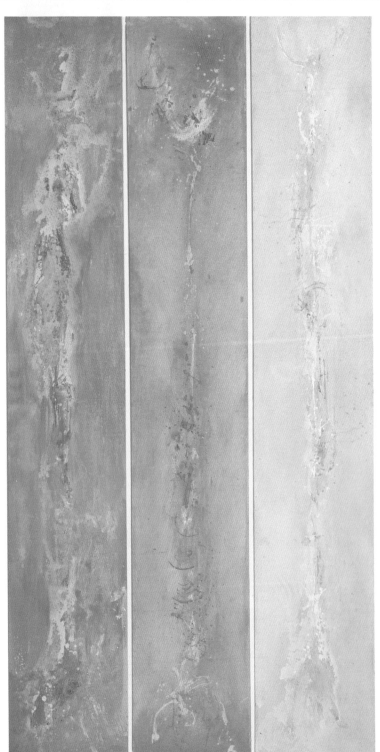

Triple Goddess 1989 (Photograph by Mike Davidson)

ARLENE
ISBISTER
MOON
MINDS
9.12.89 - 20.1.90
ABERDEEN ART GALLERY
SCHOOLHILL·ABERDEEN

TEACHER'S WHISKY
1ST EXHIBITION
AWARD
CITY OF ABERDEEN
CITY ARTS DEPARTMENT

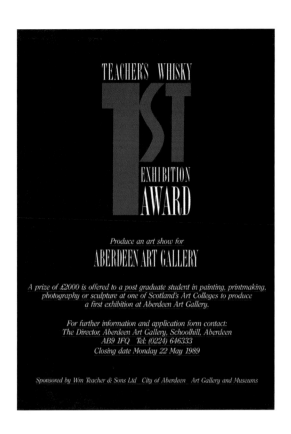

In 1995 the sailing theme was rekindled with Teacher's Round Britain Challenge – The Grand Slam of Yacht Racing – a Five Nation Championship. This was a four-leg race around the coast of Britain with two teams each from England, Scotland, Ireland and Wales and France. The teams were a mix of professional skippers and amateur sailors. The race started on 14 August and finished on 8 September. The competing boats were all Sun Fast 36s, designed by Phillipe Briand with an overall length of 37 feet 1 inch, and fitted with 8 berths.

In 1996 with the acquisition of Pedro Domecq, the holding company became Allied Domecq, the third largest wine and spirits group in the world.

Ardmore, the distinctive mainland peated single malt, at the heart of Teacher's Highland Cream, celebrated its centenary in 1998. In true Teacher's fashion the event was celebrated with a party for the staff and trade partners at the distillery. Special bottlings of 12-year and 21-year-old Ardmore were created.

'Bob' the sheepdog postcard for the New Zealand market.

1995 Postcard for the Indian market.

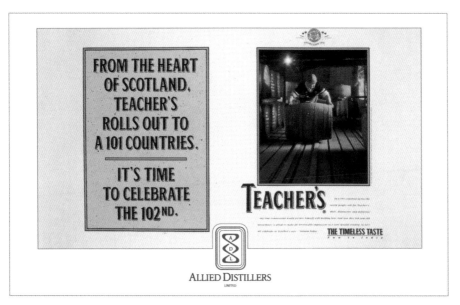

1995 Postcard celebrating the launch of Teacher's Highland Cream in India.

The late 1990s and early part of the 21st century were troubled times for Teacher's Highland Cream. Allied Domecq's priority was their number-one trademark Ballantine's Scotch Whisky. Sales of Teacher's fell below the 2 million case mark, which it had held for so long, to around 1.5 million. Teacher's, however, continued to maintain close contacts with and enjoy success in its important overseas markets.   During the last two years Teacher's Highland Cream sales have increased and are back around the 1.8 million case mark. Since 2000, India is Teacher's fastest growing market and, combined with Brazil, equates to nearly half of Teacher's global business.

Today the Teacher family is represented by Bill Bergius as Brand Heritage Director. He and other members of the Brand Heritage Department add value to Ballantine's, Teacher's and the unique malt range through three key customer services. Like his great-great-grandfather before him, Bill is passionate about Teacher's Highland Cream and indeed all things whisky.

Bill is a member of The Keepers of the Quaich Management Committee:

> *"The Keepers of the Quaich is an exclusive, internationally recognized society with members in over 60 countries worldwide. Membership, by invitation only, is granted to those with a positive record of contribution to the international success of Scotch whisky. When the society was established by the major companies (Allied Domecq is one of them) to build on the image and worldwide prestige of Scotch whisky, the industry pooled its enormous resources and strengths to promote itself with pride. All Keepers have one fundamental link in common – a love of Scotland and Scotch whisky."*

Today Bill and his wife Grace keep another Teacher interest alive, sailing their yacht *Northern Whistler* around Scotland's beautiful coast. Whenever they can their three children join them, but they have other careers and it looks as if Bill will be the last Teacher to work for the company that his great-great-grandfather, William Teacher, founded.

William Teacher would perhaps be amused to read the newspapers today. Smoking is being banned everywhere, especially in public places. For several years now passers-by in New York have seen office workers huddling in corners outside their workplaces, often in the snow, having a quick smoke. This phenomenon is spreading around the world and the smoking ban is affecting bars, restaurants and public houses.

At the same time, we are seeing a revival of Teacher's Tipsy Regulations, as licensees are being urged to clamp down on serving drunken customers. The UK government announced at the beginning of 2005 that bar staff serving underage customers and those worse for drink would be fined. The Glasgow Licensing Authorities, who were so often a thorn in William Teacher's side but applauded his no-treating rule, have clamped down on minimum pricing, happy hours and rogue operators. The effect has been to encourage consumers to look at quality rather than quantity – I like to think William would applaud this – and to enjoy a more comfortable drinking experience.

The world is still not at peace, and injustices abound. We have not yet achieved the better world, which both the Chartist Movement and Unitarian Churches wished to achieve in the 19th century. William was a member of both of these organisations. But I think William Teacher would approve of the better standard of living and shorter working hours enjoyed by the majority of the population in the UK. I am sure he would be proud of his descendants and the great success achieved by them and Teacher's Highland Cream Perfection of Old Scotch Whisky.

As I write these closing paragraphs at the end of July 2005, Allied Domecq has been bought by Pernod Richard of France and Fortune Brands of the USA. With continued interest in the brand I am confident of one thing: Teacher's Highland Cream will continue to satisfy consumer taste for an uncompromising, distinctive, richly flavoured Scotch whisky.

Allied Domecq is focusing on Teacher's Highland Cream to coincide with its 175th birthday with a new advertising and promotional campaign and the new bottle design featured at the beginning of this book. And the theme is "Scotch The Way We Like It" – we know William Teacher would certainly have approved of this slogan.

So let's drink the health of this very special 175-year-old Teacher's Highland Cream whisky, which is one of the finest, most distinctive, flavourful blends on the market.

Slainte Mhath!